WOMEN MAKING HISTORY

BLACK WOMEN IN BRITAIN

JACQUELINE HARRIOTT

B. T. Batsford Ltd   London

Acknowledgements

Cover illustrations
The black and white illustration shows women from the West Indies arriving in Southampton in 1952, (Topham). The colour illustration shows a barrister in chambers, (Sally and Richard Greenhill).

First published 1992

Typeset by Tek-Art Ltd, West Wickham, Kent
and printed in Great Britain
by BPCC Hazell Books
Alylesbury, Bucks
for the publishers
B. T. Batsford Ltd
4 Fitzhardinge Street
London W1H 0AH

ISBN 0 7134 6286 8

It's taken several years to put this book together. My thanks go to my dear mother, my two children who patiently stood by, Valerie who believed in me all the way and the many special women who made this possible. A special thanks goes to the women who agreed to be interviewed for this book.

The comments and opinions expressed in this book are my own. While every effort has been made to provide accurate information, I do not assume and hereby disclaim any liability to any party for loss or damage caused by errors or omission in this book.

The Author and Publishers would like to thank the following for permission to reproduce illustrations: Robert F. Brien: Map on page 7; The British Library: fig. 1; Camden Black Sisters: fig. 11a; The Collection of the Earl of Mansfield, Scone Palace, Perth: Fig. 2; Roshini Kempadoo/Format: figs. 14, 22a; Raissa Page/Format: figs. 19, 24a, 25; Brenda Price/Format: fig. 18; Suzanne Roden/Format: fig. 11; Sally and Richard Greenhill: figs. 7a, 9, 10, 23, 23a; The Hulton Picture Co.: figs. 4, 5, 6, 7, 8, 12, 13, 17a, 22, 29; The Imperial War Museum: figs. 15, 16, 21; Virago Press: fig. 24. The pictures were researched by David Pratt.

Contents

Introduction

Introduction – Setting the Scene

lack people. What does that bring to your mind – slaves, Africa, racism, reggae, riots, mugging, menial work, athletes? In short, it can sound and feel like problems. Many white British people still see black people in Britain as their subordinates and therefore not citizens with the same rights and opportunities. In fact, black people, and especially black women, have had a long and close connection with Britain, at all levels of society.

If you take the time to try and explore this part of British history the traditional channels of information, for example, history books, don't include a true record of events. You might stumble upon occasional evidence of their presence and the odd picture in a text, which do not faithfully represent the extent of their contribution to the economic, social and political framework of the society in which we live.

Black women need no introduction for their presence; they have earned it. They continue to contribute to shaping the consciousness of our inner city communities and Britain at large.

People from Africa and Asia and their descendants have been living in Britain for over 500 years. Their

To be SOLD,

A Black Girl, the Property of John Bull, Eleven Years of Age, who is extremely handy works at her Needle tolerably, and speaks English perfectly well; is of an excellent Temper, and willing Disposition.

Enquire of Mrs. Owen, at the Angel Inn, behind St. Clement's Church in the Strand.

1 An advertisement from the Public Advertiser, *28 November 1769*

presence grew to be particularly significant during the sixteenth century. Today more than 50 per cent of black people living here were born in Britain.

In the fifteenth century it was not uncommon to see black people as slaves, domestic servants and 'play things' of the upper classes and fashionable people of the time. Though largely concentrated in London, by the second half of the seventeenth century black people were scattered all over Britain. Some of those enslaved were able to run away and free themselves from the hard life of bondage. On becoming free some managed to obtain an education and were able to move up in society. It was then that the beginnings of black middle class developed. Many never got this opportunity and remained as slaves – oppressed and exploited by the host country.

Black women were often found in domestic service, having survived the rigours and bad conditions of an Atlantic crossing through the notorious Middle Passage and slave market. Indian women, too, worked as laundry maids, cooks and personal servants. On gaining their freedom, some worked their passage back to their home country, like this woman who advertised in the *Daily Advertiser* of 17 November 1773: 'A Female Black Servant would be glad to wait on any Lady or Children going to India: she came from thence . . .'

By the twentieth century, in large sea ports such as Cardiff and Liverpool, black communities had developed. During the First World War there was a boom for black labour. But after the war, demobilized white seamen returned to claim their old jobs and black seamen faced unemployment. Some, however,

2 Dido Elizabeth Lindsay and Lady Elizabeth Mary Murray (1779). Dido was the daughter of Sir John Lindsay and an African slave

managed to keep their jobs, causing deep resentment among the whites. The hostility resulted in race riots in 1919. Black and white men and women fought openly on the streets. Black people were made to feel guilty for daring to defend themselves against the lynch mob. Throughout the 1920s and '30s there was severe unemployment in Britain. Life for black people was extremely difficult and hazardous. Black women, in particular, underwent a period of great hardship, aggravated by the desparate need to find work. Those black women who found jobs during this time had to work very long hours and were often exhausted to preserve whatever little they could get.

The 1950s saw the start of the biggest immigration of black people to Britain. It is on these women and their second generation daughters that this book concentrates. The experiences of some of these women, their daughters and granddaughters need to be shared as part of an oral history experience. Black history has traditionally been a spoken one, passed down from mothers to daughters over the generations.

What follows are profiles of eight black women; women who live, work and continue to struggle for the best they can achieve and deserve. Each has a different experience of her reception in the host country and each has channelled her energies in different areas.

Often, it is easier to ignore problems and issues which do not touch us personally. But sometimes, when we become aware of what the individuals involved have to say, we realize that we can learn from their experience.

From the 1920s to the present black women have

continued to play their part in bringing about change in Britain. We don't always want to recognize the commitment of these women; much less their contribution to and position in the society of which they are a part. Sometimes our attention is caught by the few famous individuals who step into the spotlight for a brief moment. Now, people are being made more aware of parts of black women's history – through books and the media. But even now, when we hear about what a particular woman did, said or wrote, her achievements seem surprising. Why is this?

For me, it is very important that both young men and women gain an appreciation of black women and a respect for their contributions both in and outside the home. Without this education, we should not be surprised if our young adults, both black and white, go through all their formative years with the notion that black women could never in a hundred years be involved in wars, become leaders or engage themselves in activities which men usually dominated. Furthermore, there may be reservations about black women's abilities and the appropriateness of black women's full participation in our society and workforce.

Understanding something of the day-to-day struggles and achievements of black women can have a positive effect on asserting our equality, rights and plans for the future. It is, I think, easier for black women to expand their horizons to include the non-traditional possibilities when they know that black women have become leaders, political activists, writers, doctors, academics creative artists, self-employed business people . . . the list is endless. Young

black women of today need to know that their aspirations are not strange and new but rather part of a tradition of black women throughout the world. Angela Davis, Afro-American writer, political activist and lecturer, reminds us in her classic black feminist narrative, *Women, Race and Class,* that 'black women simply express in their own way the spirit of strength and perseverance'.

The book is divided into eight sections, each of which gives you the opportunity to explore through a particular theme some social and political history issues. There is no reason why young adults of all ethnic groups should not use this material to explore wider issues related to Equal Opportunities, Race and Class. Participation in the activities in this book should help readers to:

learn about themselves, their country, their communities

plan for a future which involves an appreciation and consideration of their world and its people

explore the issues and testimonies which interest them by talking with each other and to other people

develop survival skills and career success styles which will build their confidence and enhance their ability to live independent lives

share information and experiences with others who have similar concerns and interests

understand the historical, current and future perspectives of black women.

Just As A Start

Write down all the groups you can think of which have migrated to Britain:

- between AD 0 and 1800
- between 1800 and 1945
- after 1945.

Look at the map and mark their countries of origin.

When do you think they came to Britain? Can you

suggest an exact date on the map beside the country of origin?

Have you ever had to move home or move to another part of the country or to a new country altogether? If you or your family have never had to make this kind of move, think of a friend or relative who has and try and answer the questions.

- When was it that you or your family moved to .... ?   (Fill in the name of the place.)

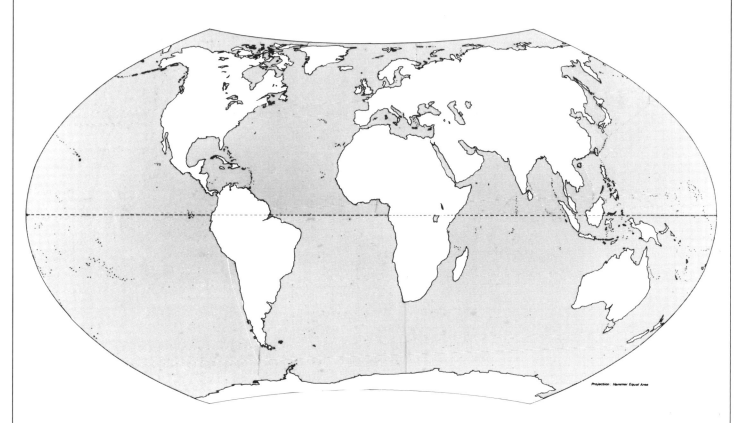

- What were the reasons for you or your family to move?

- What did you gain by moving away?

- What did you lose?

- In what ways do you think you had to adapt?

- What things would you not be prepared to change or give up as a result of moving away?

- If you were asked where you came from, what would you answer? Why?

- Do you think people who migrate to Britain should adapt to the British way of doing things?

CHAPTER 1

Black Women and Work

Agatha (b. 1932)

Agatha is from Grenada. She came to Britain in 1957. She was one of the many women who came to Britain to join their husbands during the 1950s. Agatha's husband had come to Britain a year before and had found work and accommodation.

3 Agatha

Agatha had three children that she left behind when she decided to come over to Britain. 'Back home' she had enjoyed doing embroidery, a skill taught to her by her mother. She was able to attract a small income by taking in work from customers – and did not need to travel out of the home to find work. Her paid job helped to maintain her family as there were hardly any State benefits in Grenada. When she left for Britain she was able to leave her children with their grandmother, who already lived with the family.

There was no doubt in her mind about joining her husband, no dread about what she would find, only a determined spirit to travel the 7000 miles and be with him. The journey was made in a boat called the *Ipeania*, which went first to Barcelona. Agatha had an overnight stay at a guest house in Spain, where she could not speak or understand the language. She went onwards by train, through France. 'One minute you were going forward then the next backwards', she recalls. 'It was all so confusing and tiring. There were a lot of us.'

Messages that had been relayed back to the people in Grenada were that England was paved with gold. Agatha believed that her dreams would be made true and that she would perhaps pluck that nugget of gold from the pavements.

When she arrived she was met with a dismal picture of industrial Britain – towering chimneys billowing out dark grey smoke, a memory which has remained embedded in her mind as her very first impression of Britain.

Kenneth, a black man from Jamaica, and his wife, a white English woman, owned a tenement house which

4 New arrivals from the Caribbean on the boat train to London

they rented out to newly arrived migrants.

Many white landlords and landladies were very much against taking in black tenants, both because of their own racist attitudes and for fear of what the neighbours might say. Newly arrived immigrants were not eligible for a council house and were left to their own devices in a strange country to find their own housing. Rents paid by black people were very high.

Agatha recalls:

Me and my husband lived in one room on the ground floor. The furnished room served as the bedroom, the kitchen, the bathroom, the sitting room, with joint use of the toilet with other tenants in the house.

This was the home that she and her husband remained in for the next four years. During this time they saved hard in order to buy their own house and escape the damp and cold conditions, at the same time as supporting their children at home in Grenada. Many migrants looking for a house to buy were exploited by estate agents who directed them into areas in towns and cities where less attractive properties were to be found.

It was around this time that I found myself pregnant and I returned to Grenada to my children and to give birth to my child there. Two years later, with my children and husband, I returned to Britain and settled in Sheffield. My baby had contracted meningitis and this had left the child mentally handicapped and put a strain on the family. I remained at home for a short period but then found part-time work in a factory. Working a twilight shift, I could be at home for the children on their return from school then work from five o'clock to ten o'clock in the evening.

My salary was £8 per week in the late 1960s. With my husband's wage I was able to manage. Life was good. A move to a full-time job as a waitress in a hospital gave me a small wage increase but working conditions became unbearable when a white woman was installed over my head and I was overlooked for promotion. Furthermore, this newcomer was receiving a higher wage. This injustice

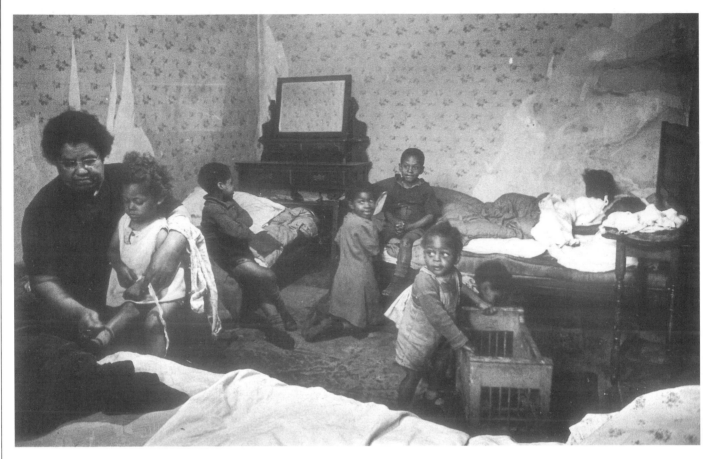

5 Newly-arrived families were often forced to live in very poor housing

infuriated me so I terminated my contract. It was clear that I was rejected because of unfair discrimination but there was nowhere for me to take up my grievance and get some justice.

She moved into a variety of unskilled manual jobs in the service industries, experiencing long and often unsociable hours, poor prospects and low pay.

Any form of discrimination and hostility open or hidden I would not be tolerating. I never took my problems to the union wherever I worked.

Unions at that time were not interested in defending the rights of black people at work.

Little notice was taken by my employers and for the last 18 years of working in the same job I seldom lean on anyone for support, recognition, or approval for what I do. I am very competent at carrying out my job and have had many years of experience in learning how to survive. I have come to the conclusion that my existence is dependent on harnessing my own personal survival skills and fighting my own battles. I recognize the inequality between black and white workers in job level and job conditions. There is no use complaining. Nothing is ever done.

Questions

1 What expectations did Agatha have of life in Britain? Why did she believe this?
2 What problems did Agatha encounter in Britain and how did she cope with them?
3 Why do you think Agatha never took her problems at work to the union?

6 *Black women in the 1940s and 1950s took low-paid manual jobs*

Something She Had to Do

The growth of the British economy since the sixteenth century has depended on the cheap labour provided in the colonies and on the immigration of workers from the poorer parts of Europe and the colonies to Britain's industrial cities, such as London, Manchester, Liverpool, Birmingham and Bristol. During the nineteenth century, the majority of immigrants came from Ireland to build the canals and railways. Other refugees from Europe, in particular Jewish and Ukranians, provided an additional boost to the labour force. The whole system was in place to deliberately attract people into Britain whenever labour was needed. At other times the flow of labour was discouraged. The 1905 Aliens Act was implemented by the British government to actively control the immigration of Ukranians, Jews and others who wanted to enter Britain.

Until the early 1950s America was the country where many black people, especially from the Caribbean, chose to settle. It was closer to the Caribbean, warmer than Britain and economically richer. It already had a well-established black community. In 1952 the American Congress passed the McCarren Walter Act, which restricted immigration of British West Indians to the USA. The number allowed into the country was reduced from 65,000 a year to 800. As a result, the migration of black people was shifted away from America to other parts of the world. At that time Britain had an 'open door' policy which gave all Commonwealth citizens the status of British citizenship.

It was an obvious choice for many people from Commonwealth countries to come to Britain, especially as there was a labour shortage there which

7 The National Health Service solved its problem of labour shortages by recruiting in the Caribbean

lured many to the so-called 'Mother Country' in the late forties and fifties. Many women that I spoke to about how Britain was portrayed to them back in their countries of origin were led to believe that it was the mother country, the promised land, a place where opportunities were to be found, where the streets were paved with gold, where there were jobs for all and nobody went without. As children, many had celebrated the coronation of their British King and Queen and celebrated in traditional ways other national holidays to remain loyal to Britain and its colonies. There was a real sense of patriotism and solidarity felt by everyone in the Commonwealth.

Labour shortages meant that there were many jobs in Britain. British workers had the opportunity of choosing less tedious work with better pay, conditions and prospects. Shortages were particularly noticeable in semi-skilled and unskilled manual jobs that white workers were no longer prepared to do. Black migrant workers were taken on to fill the vacancies.

Recruitment campaigns were organized by Britain in many Caribbean countries to attract workers for the National Health Service, bus crews for London Transport and workers for the hotel and catering industry. Despite the attractive campaigns, these jobs were low-paid shift work, permanent night shifts or with poor conditions. They were frequently in the older, declining industries. Racism and discrimination reduced the job opportunities and promotion prospects for many black people. The more skilled and professional black workers were therefore forced into jobs below their level of qualification.

White workers must have realized that black workers were coming in to do the menial work that they had previously done – and for the same low wage. But white workers were often indifferent and could be abusive, like the London bus driver who said, 'You can't tell one from another, they all look the same to me'. All black workers experienced racist abuse and insults were common.

Many women came to Britain to join their husbands or relatives. Others came on their own initiative in response to the employment opportunities. From the mid-1950s through to the early 1960s the proportion of

women entering Britain rose. The census of 1961 shows that a rising number of black and Asian people from the Commonwealth were living in Britain.

Working conditions for black women were particularly unattractive. They worked long hours for very low pay. They were also subject to the traditional restrictions on women at work. These restrictions applied not only to their behaviour on the job but also to what they were allowed to do during their own time away from work. Many women who worked held down two jobs: they had to do the housework and look after the children at home while working on a paid job as well. The emotional pressure was enormous. Many black women who worked were limited to institutionalized housework – cleaning, laundry work and chambermaiding. These jobs were an extension of the work black women had done under British rule in the colonies. The alternative was to work in unskilled jobs in a factory. Some women had no option but to work in this sector of employment.

Evidence

A slums . . . the houses are either not well built or are in bad repair . . . . The dock area lies low and is damp . . . . Five or six families may share a six roomed house, with a common staircase, one lavatory and one tap which may be even outside . . . . Rooms are often small . . . ventilation is rarely good and sometimes the walls are verminous . . . . It is noteworthy that children of coloured men almost always appear well fed and are warmly dressed in spite of poverty.
(Nancie Hare, 'The Prospects for Coloured Children in England', *The Keys*, July-September 1937, quoted in Peter Fryer, *Staying Power: The History of Black People in Britain*, Pluto Press, 1984)

B Wendy: In traditional societies it's hard for women but, for our mothers, working there may be better than the hard work here, for low wages. And they miss their families, their way of life. Either way they get oppressed. I would like to go back to Jamaica but with qualifications, and a job.
(M. Mac An Ghaill, *Young, Gifted and Black*, Oxford University Press, 1988)

C There were adverts everywhere: 'Come to the mother country! The mother country needs you!' That's how I learned the opportunity was here. I felt stronger loyalty towards England. There was more emphasis there than loyalty to your own island . . . . It was really the mother country and being

away from home wouldn't be that terrible because you would belong.
(West Indian woman, quoted in Elyse Dodgson, *West Indian Women to Britain in the 1950s*, Heinemann Educational, 1984)

D White women are also poor, and this is what Black women have seen by immigrating to England . . . . Women's lack of money is international. As women we produce workers for the wars, we produce workers for the factories, the mines – for all the dangerous but profit-making industries of the world. For without our well cared for, able-bodied children – the past and future workers of society – there wouldn't be a British Empire or French Empire or Dutch Empire or whatever Empire, and there wouldn't be these multi-corporations.

So when Black women come to Britain, the U.S. or any other metropolitan countries – the countries where the money is – we are here, there, for the money, not the weather. And when our children refuse to take on low-paid dirty jobs, when mothers refuse to work at home without being paid, when women refuse to take second jobs with long hours, poor equipment, dirty work – it is out of struggles that have gone on for hundreds of years that we are refusing to continue working for free or for a pittance.
(Norma Steele, 'We're in Britain for the money', Margaret Prescod-Roberts and Norma Steele, *Black Women: Bringing It All Back Home*, Falling Wall Press, 1980)

Questions

1 How does the housing described in A compare with Agatha's living conditions? Had anything changed between 1937 and 1950?

2 What were the expectations of people coming to Britain from overseas in the 1950s? In reality, what did they find and how were they treated?

3 Imagine what it was like in the 1950s and 1960s. What kinds of jobs were available for black women?

4 What restrictions and attitudes did black women face (a) when looking for work (b) at their place of work? How do you think they were affected by this treatment?

5 Is there high unemployment in your area? Do you think it is still hard for ethnic minority people to get the jobs they are qualified to do?

6 Find out about the Race Relations Act of 1976. How does it affect the way employers treat women and ethnic minority groups at work?

CHAPTER 2

Black Women and Education

Jan McKenley (b. 28 November 1955)

Jan was born in 1955 in Brixton, South London, of Jamaican parents. Her parents had met on a cruiser which was on its way across the Atlantic to Britain. Her early days were spent in the South London suburb which at that time had a small but established West Indian community. A few years later, after the birth of her

sister, her father took the family north. This was as a result of his firm moving away. They were offered housing in a suburb of Manchester, Ashton-Under-Lyme.

They were the only black family in the street. It was not until they were moving out of the area that Jan saw another black family moving into this small community. Although hers was the only black face to be seen when she played with the other kids in her road or in the playground of her primary school, the only memory she has of racism was the odd time other children taunted her by name calling. But she was left unscathed by this early display of racism and often participated in tomboy games or rode her bike with the other children who lived in her road. Roads then were free of cars.

Her days at primary school during the early 1960s were happy and painfree. Her form teacher quickly recognized that she was a bright child with potential and made arrangements with the headteacher to move Jan into a class a year ahead of her age group. Very early on in her primary school experience, positive messages and expectations were being made by other people to affirm her self-worth which in turn increased her self-confidence. It had nothing to do with her being different, but it was about her as an individual and the potential she had. She never had the feeling that being black was in any way a problem or restriction.

Her primary school was offering to her what all children irrespective of class, creed, colour or gender deserve, the equality of opportunity to achieve their full potential and the empowerment to change the course of their lives.

7a Black women are becoming a major force in education

8 Black children often found themselves in poor schools

Education was very important to Jan's family. They saw it as the mechanism which would move not only Jan but her family and community forward.

They returned to London to live with a close relative. Jan's younger brother had developed an asthmatic condition and it was felt by doctors that a move from Manchester would improve his treatment. Things did change.

Jan went to the local junior school in North London. As at the school in Manchester, it became clear that she was ahead of her contemporaries and she was again moved into a higher class. She took the eleven plus examination a year before her eleventh birthday and went on to a grammar school where she was placed in the top stream.

Many of the black children in the North London area were directed to the local secondary modern school which had an atrocious reputation. It was known as a place where girls got pregnant not where you received a formal education. Schools in the areas where a large conurbation of black people lived often had a bad name. They were usually badly resourced and staffed by indifferent teachers who did what they could under the circumstances.

Jan's parents were quite clear about what they wanted for their children. Their daughter remained in the top stream throughout her secondary school career. When her school, like most others in the 1970s, went comprehensive she continued to achieve in all areas. When it came to deciding what to do after leaving school, Jan automatically assumed that she would go on to university. She was given little advice

9 For some, school provided a path to advancement

by her teachers but this made no difference; she took her future into her own hands, and went to a university in East Anglia to take European studies. She still thinks that, with the right advice and channelling, she could have gone to Oxbridge.

Her time at university was a liberating period of her life. The Black Power movement was very much alive in the seventies and helped give black people the confidence to accept themselves as they were. It raised their expectations and encouraged them to hold on to their blackness by wearing their hair in 'Afro' styles and dressing in clothes styled to emphasize their philosophy. The 'black is beautiful' liberation spread to young black people all over the world. They gained self respect and a positive identity from recognizing that white values were not the only true values. This liberation was much needed to counteract the low self-esteem and damaged self-respect black people had experienced.

> I met a number of other black students who had come from London. I felt a sense of security and stability. The black friends that I made were my intellectual and academic peers and there was a lot of recognition and acceptance of my own position and individuality. It was a time of life skills acquisition and new experiences. I hold very happy memories of that period in my life.

After leaving university Jan took a post-graduate secretarial course at a London polytechnic. It was something that she would fall back on later on in her life. She worked in a variety of jobs over the next couple of years, but she finally veered towards training to become a teacher. This decision was based on the

10 In the 1970s young black people began to develop their own style – to express their 'blackness'

experiences from her own school days. It would also please her parents to have Jan be a teacher.

At the same time, Jan became interested in the Women's Liberation Movement (Feminism), particularly the issue of abortion rights. She became a counsellor and a campaigner. Through this work she found herself moving into education as a student services officer in a North London further education college in Stoke Newington. It was a job which brought her into contact with students from different backgrounds. She could monitor their grievances, as well as be a listening and supportive ear to them when they arrived at her door with their problems.

I was one of a very small number of black staff in the college at that time. It was evident that the black students in the college had been starved of positive role models. I was inundated with casework and appointments for students. I also worked part-time in the evenings as a youth worker.

She soon realized that her liberated punk image and

feminist ideas did not necessarily match the identity that her black community needed to find then. She made the important decision to go for a more conventional image. Looking back, she still feels it was the appropriate thing to do as an open gesture to her black community and all the positive things that it believed in and was trying to achieve at that time.

Jan moved on to do something different in the college. A job as a careers education officer was offered to her for which she took a two-year post-graduate teacher training course. During this time she had a daughter but still went on and completed her course.

Her experience as a part-time youth worker provided Jan with a new dimension to her work. An officer of the Department of Education and Science invited her to serve on an important committee which was to look at the provision of the Youth Service throughout the country. She was the only black person sitting on that committee and took the opportunity to be a representative of her community and bring awareness to the other members of the committee. From this she moved into a boys' school as a senior teacher and stayed there for three years.

She returned to the college in Stoke Newington, this time taking up a senior lecturer post. Her job involved having collective responsibility for curriculum and staff development but with a particular bias towards racial issues. She built on and developed other interests and skills in the area of training people to be personnel and senior managers.

It was not long before Jan's career path would take another upward turn, this time moving outside the educational framework to which she had been loyal for ten years.

I applied for a position with a private industrial training consultancy. There were 220 applicants of which three were appointed. Two of those recruited were black. I was one of them. It was one of the few occasions that I had been appointed alongside another black person to a job of equal status and merit. I felt pleasantly exhilarated and excited to be getting the chance to work alongside a black colleague who had got through the same rigorous selection process as myself. We would also be able to offer each other support and comradeship.

A year went by and the opportunity to move on arose again. Jan was motivated by her strong conviction that by moving back into education she might assist in bringing about some minor changes. She was appointed as Her Majesty's Inspector for schools.

My role is about being a black HMI. That means I am not afraid to declare my blackness first and my HMI role second. Furthermore, I am the youngest HMI appointed to date.

Jan has been a consumer of education and has delivered the service in all its phases as a teacher and youth worker, a trainer in education and finally in the support, monitoring, advising and planning role of an HMI. Having gone through the many aspects of the educational service she is left with no doubt that the quality of education she received should be the entitlement of every child. It goes without saying that our schools have an obligation to offer the opportunities for every black child, as well as white, to take the best and have claim to an education which sets them up **for life**, just like Jan's experience.

Questions

1 From early on in her life Jan had a very positive sense of who she was and what she was capable of doing. Where did these messages come from?

2 What was different about the way many other black children were feeling and being treated in schools in other parts of Britain at that time?

3 Why do you think the issue of a 'good' education was particularly important to Jan and her family living in Britain?

4 From what you have read about Jan, why do you think she has been so successful in her career?

Irrespective of Race

Black women have always recognized the importance of education as a way of liberating themselves and their children from poverty and putting themselves on the ladder to getting an interesting job and social mobility. Many black women in the Caribbean, India and Africa made enormous sacrifices to send their children to school, despite the fact that the education received was often at a basic level, to acquire the skills of reading and writing. For some it stopped at 14 years old but, depending on the country, it was sometimes much earlier. The education system throughout the Commonwealth was based on the European style and inevitably had a 'white bias'.

Religious and charitable organizations ran schools throughout the Commonwealth to educate its youngsters. A small handful of the brightest black children won scholarships and were given the once in a lifetime opportunity of receiving higher education which would offer them the chance of a profession. Thus the achievement levels of pupils were high as they were keen to do well. Teachers were respected and held in awe. The desire for an education and all the positive things that it offers has remained with us.

Black children who arrived in Britain in the 1950s and 60s did not find the inner city classrooms at all attractive or happy places to be. Firstly, many of the children had been uprooted from their homes and brought to Britain to join their mothers and families.

11 In the 1990s black women are developing their skills to improve their chances of getting a fair slice of the job market

Secondly, they quickly had to try and adapt to a new system of schooling in a strange country which had different ways of doing things. Thirdly, the education system was not geared to acknowledge that the needs of some children were different and that perhaps its educational policies and ethos should be reviewed. Consequently, black children were isolated and made to appear as failures and delinquents in most aspects of their school life, apart from sporting activities.

> They only wanted us to play their sports. They always did that to us. We felt intimidated and some girls were punished for not fulfilling the white teachers' dreams.
> (Cheryl Thomas, secondary school experience in Clapham)

Their unresponsive, uninterested behaviour led teachers to believe that black children were unintelligent at the best of times and hostile, aggressive and difficult to control at the worst. Tracey Wilmott, looking back on her junior school in Battersea, South London, says, 'Sometimes I felt teachers picked on me. It was an easy way out for them'. Is it any wonder that pupils felt alienated, when the school curriculum and environment were inadequate to meet the educational needs of all the children who attended the schools? Jennifer Williams found that the teachers in Birmingham in the 1960s responded to the presence of black children by:

putting over a certain set of values (Christian), a code of behaviour (middle class), a set of academic and job aspirations in which white collar workers have higher prestige than manual, clean jobs than dirty.
('The younger generation', in John Rex and Robert Moore (eds), *Race, Community and Conflict*, Oxford University Press, 1967)

Today, younger black people have levels of qualifications that are much more like their white counterparts but not identical. More young black adults educated in the UK have a tendency to stay on in full-time education after the ages of 16 and 18, and more black women are studying part-time for academic and vocational qualifications. As a consequence, the misleading stereotypes of the 1950s and 60s are gradually being squashed, although many do still persist today.

Throughout Britain more and more women are taking the opportunity to return to work after bringing up children. Some are returning to education, either to get vocational training or to follow a traditional course of study at a college or university. Black women are part of this overall trend. They are improving their skills and getting the appropriate education to support and widen their chances of getting a fair slice of the job market.

Evidence

A You remember the lady I told you about who said how refreshing it was that I *admit* it [being black], I told her when I left, when I knew, of course, there wouldn't be any job, I said, 'Black people are just black people. And some of us, like me, we have very simple ideas about what we want to do. I want to teach. *You*,' I told her, 'you want me to be the MP from my district, or an ambassador. But I don't want to do that. I just want to teach children, preferably little ones, and I don't want to teach them about politics or race. I want to teach them to read and write and work with numbers. Why can't you understand that?' That's what I told her . . . . So you know what she says to me, and she's smiling all the time I'm talking, she says, 'You know, Miss Cressy, you'd make a great ambassador. Have you ever thought of foreign service work?'
(Eleanor Cressy, looking back on an interview for a teaching job, quoted in Thomas J. Cottle, *Black Testimony: Voices of Britain's West Indians*, Wildwood House, 1978)

B The impact of unsuitable books like *Janet and John*, *Little Black Sambo* and others reinforced the white stereotypes and probably had the effect of limiting the horizons of young black boys and girls.
(Dorothy Hunt reflects on her days as a primary school teacher in the 1960s.)

C Education is not about allowing us to realise our full potential; it is not about encouraging us to exercise our minds to the full or creating self-aware individuals. Rather the education system seeks to grade and discipline the majority of school leavers for the world of work outside. With our understanding of the jobs black people do, it is obvious what kind of education we are going to get; we do the worse jobs in society and are well prepared for this by receiving the worse kind of education.
(Conference of OWAAD (The Organization of Women of Asian and African Descent), March 1979, quoted in Gaby

Weiner (ed.), *Just a Bunch of Girls*, Open University Press, 1985)

D You can't get jobs. There should be jobs, but it depends on the employer as well. He might be one of those who doesn't like blacks. I mean, if a white person and a black person went to the same school and got the same degrees, the white person is more entitled to get it than the black. I mean, we're all classed as stupid.

(School girl, quoted in *Multiracial Education*, vol. 10, No. 5, Summer 1982)

E For most teachers the primary cause of black youths' problems lies in the black community itself. So, the solution lies in black youth changing and adapting to the school's demands. (Hall *et al, A Different Reality*, 1986)

Questions

1 In A, what problems did Eleanor Cressy face when looking for a teaching job? What assumptions did the woman interviewing her make about her because of her race?

2 What do B and C have to say about the kind of education received by black children? How is their education different from that of white children?

3 What assumptions is the girl quoted in D making about employers? Do you think she is right?

4 Do you agree with the statement made in E?

5 It was suggested by the government in the 1960s that children from overseas experiencing difficulties in schools were suffering from 'culture shock'. What do you think was meant by this? In what other areas might they have felt it?

CHAPTER 3

Black Women and Trade Unions

Claudia Jones (1915-1964)

laudia Jones was a black woman activist in the 1950s and early 60s, committed to the Trade Union principle. She was born in a country ruled by the British colonial government. Trinidad was part of the British West Indies. The Trinidadian people were poor and survived under difficult circumstances. At that time white plantation owners still lived in a grand and comfortable style. Claudia's parents worked hard; they had dreams of leaving Trinidad for a better life in America. When they had got enough money for the fare together the whole family moved to the United States. Claudia was 8 years old. There was a large number of people from Africa in America. They had been there since the days of slavery. Claudia's family settled in Harlem which had become a significant cultural area for black people. The Universal Negro Improvement Association had its headquarters there, led by a man called Marcus Garvey.

Claudia's family found their position little changed in America. They experienced overt racism at work, in education and housing. 'Jim Crow' racism was the term used to describe the racial situation in America. White people had the best housing, and jobs with good salaries, while the black 'folk' lived in poor, slum conditions and were forced to work long unsociable hours for very little pay. Claudia's family paid the ultimate price for having to tolerate such conditions for Claudia's mother died at work over her sewing machine. The family were sorely angered and bitter with the system, which they had no alternative but to be part of and endure.

Soon after her mother's death Claudia left school to look for work. She did not find this an easy task as 'Jim Crow' racism was still in operation. Claudia Jones recognized that her people were being treated badly despite the fact that black labour was needed to support the economy. She joined the Youth Communist League at the age of 18. In her twenties she already had a clear understanding of politics. She

11a Claudia Jones

became determined 'to develop an understanding of the sufferings of my people and my class and to look for a way forward to end them'. She took up responsibility for the Women's Communist Commission and encouraged black women to campaign for their rights. At this time she worked for a black newspaper during the day and the Women's Commission in the evenings. She was also studying to be an actress in whatever spare time she had left.

In 1939 the Second World War broke out. Claudia continued to work to improve the lives of poor, working-class people. She was very committed to her work and the struggle for political change. By 1941 she was a full-time politician. It was during this time that she wrote about Adolf Hitler, saying that there should be no compromise with him because he believed in slavery. She stated that everyone was fighting in the war together and there was no need for race hatred. She yearned for a united front.

After the war, in 1945, black people were treated as before. All the black heroes were forgotten. The ghettos reemerged, jobs were as low paid as ever and employment for black women restricted. The majority of black women worked in domestic service, and had not yet organized themselves into trade unions. As a dedicated communist, Claudia Jones believed that socialism held the only promise of liberation for black women. She knew that part of the struggle was to encourage her white colleagues to get rid of the racist and sexist attitudes that were holding black women back.

In the early 1950s, more and more black people were making their voices heard through the Communist Party (CP), which was prepared to defend working-class people, black and white. The American government felt threatened and passed a number of legislative rulings against the CP and immigrants. This time became known as the McCarthy Era because it was Senator McCarthy who claimed that members of the CP were trying to overthrow the government. He instigated a 'witch hunt' in which many thousands of people from all walks of life were suspected and tried for being Communists. During this period a lot of people were sent to jail. The trials were a travesty of justice as the juries were biased and witnesses were paid to give false evidence.

Claudia Jones was arrested in 1953 and convicted of 'un-American activities'. She was by this time so admired for her commitment to the Communist ideals and her position as a leader within the party that a campaign was set up to have her acquitted. Appeals went on until 1955 when she was finally jailed. Segregation even occurred in the prison where she was held. She was separated from her white friends and comrades.

When Claudia was released later that year, she was deported. She came to Britain because her native Trinidad would not have her back. The colonial government there was too afraid of what she might do. Just before she left America, Paul Robeson, a famous singer and close colleague of Claudia's, gave a farewell speech. He said:

> Claudia belongs to us, belongs to America, and the reactionaries in power who have ordered her deportation have thereby delivered another grievous blow against the best interests of our country. Along with millions of others who came to these shores from all parts of the world, Claudia has enriched our land, and the best of America is her rightful heritage.

On arrival in Britain, Claudia continued her political activity to improve the situation of black and Asian people here. She founded the *West Indian Gazette* in 1958. It became the main monthly newspaper for black people and was the voice in which to air grievances and inform each other about the major issues affecting the black immigrant population in Britain. By 1960 the *Gazette* had a circulation of 15,000.

In 1958, white youths committed racial attacks on black people and their homes in Notting Hill, London. After this it was Claudia who took the initiative to organize a first multiracial event – the Notting Hill Carnival in London, which still takes place every summer.

On 1 July 1962, the British government brought into effect the Commonwealth Immigrants Act. A system of vouchers was introduced giving would-be immigrants high priority if they had a specific job to come to and little chance of entry if not. In effect, this Act heavily restricted immigration. For Claudia, this was a repetition of the McCarthy Era and again she witnessed the same frustration and anger of black people that she had seen in America. She continued to campaign and was invited as an opening speaker to trade union conferences and meetings all over Britain and the world.

Claudia Jones was a well-respected black woman and an admired politician. She believed strongly in getting rid of the division and alienation of black people in the work place and worked towards achieving equality of opportunity. She spoke on many subjects, including peace and world issues. She put everything aside to campaign for women everywhere, even sacrificing her health. Despite a serious heart condition, she continued to campaign until 1964, when her illness claimed her life at the age of 49. Her funeral at Golders Green Crematorium was attended by crowds of people. At the head of the funeral procession a banner was carried, bearing the words: 'World People Unite for Freedom and Peace'. Claudia Jones is buried in Highgate Cemetery next to Karl Marx.

Questions

1 What did 'Jim Crow' racism mean?

2 Claudia Jones was convicted of 'un-American activities'. What do you think is meant by 'un-American'? Do you think Claudia was guilty of this?

3 Claudia believed strongly in 'equality of opportunity'. What does this mean? What evidence of this belief was there in her work in America and Britain?

Is It Treason to Reason?

The British Trade Union movement is the oldest in the world (over 300 years old) and, largely because of this, it is the most difficult to understand. There are a number of different types. Most unions began as groups of workers following a particular occupation or trade who banded together to protect their mutual interest. Some moved on to absorb other occupational unions. Black people were clearly not attracted to join unions in the 1950s and 60s. Their experience of unions in the past had made them realize that British unions were not interested in protecting their rights. The Racism Riots of 1919 in Cardiff and Liverpool had resulted from the British seamen's union choosing to sign on white foreign seamen in preference to black British ones. This state of affairs led the black seamen in Cardiff (of whom there were about 3000) to form the Coloured Colonial Seamen's Union some years later. In April 1935 two investigators from the League of Coloured Peoples spent a week in Cardiff interviewing over 200 seamen and others. They uncovered a scandal in the city. The Authorities, including the trade unions, had tricked all the black seamen to register as aliens, although they were eligible for British nationality. Due to the actions of the League of Coloured Peoples, the seamen were able to claim their rightful nationality, thus eliminating the threat of deportation. Black people were inclined to handle their own concerns.

Today, a higher percentage of black people are involved in unions than whites and, over the past ten years, women workers have become increasingly active in unions. But still, compared to the number of women in the workforce, they play only a small part in the running of unions. Black women make up about a quarter of the black worker representation in the unions. They tend to be under represented in key union jobs.

Since the 1960s the larger unions have been outspoken in condemning racism and discrimination against black people in the workplace.

There are those who believe that the unions could do much more for the black caucus who pay their subscriptions and support the prosperity of the union. Many are shop stewards but continually find that they are not given the opportunity to have a greater say in the running of the unions. Racial equality is in the interest of all trade union members. The basic principle of trade unionism is that unity is strength . . . . Trade unionists should do all they can and use every opportunity at work, in all branches, in all trades council and in local community activities to oppose

12 Even in the 1950s housing conditions for the black community in Cardiff were attrocious

those who seek to incite racial discrimination and hatred in order to divide workers and the community.
(*TUC Charter for Black Workers*, Trades Union Congress, 1981)

In the summer of 1976, one of the most unusual strikes started at the Grunwick Laboratories in North-West London. Although only a local dispute, it became international news and lasted until July 1978. It was a strike of mainly Asian workers from East Africa, most of whom were women. These women were considered to be very uncomplaining and in no way militant, but they had many grievances. One of the main problems was that they were compelled to work overtime at very short notice. The women were

upset as it forced them to neglect their children and families. Also, the very hot summer of 1976 meant that, with no suitable ventilation, conditions became difficult.

On 20 August 1976 Mrs Jayaben Desai, a middle-aged woman and perhaps Britain's best-known Asian trade unionist, was involved in a dispute with her boss, Mr Alden. She decided to walk out. As she left Mr Alden's office, she called to the other workers:

My friends, listen to this. What is happening to me today will happen to you tomorrow. This man wouldn't speak to white workers like he speaks to us. He says he is giving me the sack but I am leaving myself. I do not want to be given his sack.

13   *The Grunwick strike 1976. Mrs Jayaben Desai is on the right wearing a light-coloured coat*

Other individuals were involved in a series of disagreements and left the plant. This small group met and had vague ideas about joining a trade union and organizing a strike at Grunwick. They knew nothing about unions but went to a Citizens Advice Bureau to get information. They joined the Association for Professional, Executive, Clerical and Computer staffs (APEX). By now there were 137 people on strike. The union began to pay them strike pay.

On 2 September the strikers were sacked. Union officials attempted to negotiate with the senior manager at Grunwick. Questionnaires were sent to the workers to see if they wanted an official union. Of those sent out, 93 questionnaires were returned, all of which were in favour of APEX. The management at Grunwick, however, refused to recognize the union.

As the strike progressed, it became noticed by the national media. Many other trade union members from across the country came out in support of the Grunwick strikers, including post office workers and miners. By the summer of 1977 mass pickets were being held outside the Grunwick Laboratories. The media coverage of these pickets was often biased. The newspapers published the figures of police officers injured but ignored the many picketers who were also injured. The 11 July 1977 was a day of mass action on which 18,000 people turned up on the picket line. That evening on the BBC's *Panorama*, Margaret Thatcher said, 'I have the greatest admiration for those people on the bus who have gone through the picket line day after day'.

The government became worried by the strike and set up a Court of Inquiry under the chairmanship of Lord Justice Scarman. Many people involved in the dispute were questioned. The report was published on 25 August. It found that the workers had a real grievance and said of the largely immigrant workforce: 'They are particularly at risk when they are employed in a fiercely competitive business where low prices and rapid service bring great rewards'. Although the report was critical of the mass picketing, it recommended that

*14 A National Association of Local Government Officers
Conference*

the workers were to be reinstated by Grunwick. On
the question of union recognition, the report was not
clear-cut in its recommendations.

George Ward, the managing director of Grunwick,
rejected the Court of Inquiry's recommendations.
Mass picketing continued and on 17 October 1977 an
estimated 5000 people assembled outside Grunwick
led by Arthur Scargill. Many picketers were arrested.
On 21 November Jayaben Desai and a few others
began a hunger strike outside the Trades Union
Congress building. She said: 'I will not remove my
hunger strike from your doorstep. The problem is
you, and I want to expose you to the world'. The strike
committee had by now lost faith in the unions, which
they felt were not acting entirely in the strikers'
interests. By 1978 the strike movement was drawing to
an end, though it was not until later on in the year that
defeat was admitted.

Despite their failure to win the strike, the workers at
Grunwick had won the support and respect of the
workforce and public of Britain. There was at
Grunwick an exceptional group of Asian women
supported by black women who were determined not
to fall into the pattern of submissiveness and passivity.
They were the women who had kept the momentum of
the strike going over the months, a task which had
required tremendous commitment and determination.

Despite the Race Relations Act and equal
opportunities policies, there are still complaints of
racial abuse and sexual harassment of many black
women at work. Black workers have established a
Black Trade Unionist Solidarity Movement which has
taken notice of the contribution black women are
making to the movement.

Recently black women's groups have emerged
within certain unions like NALGO and COHSE.
Efforts by these groups have resulted in better
childcare facilities, including nurseries and playgroups
within inner city areas. They are consciously seeking
to break barriers of racism and sexism by becoming
active in trade union issues. Their long-term aim is to
secure better conditions for women workers
everywhere.

Evidence

A Outside the factory gates of Willesden, the High Road suddenly exploded into a blaze of colour. Down the road, banners flying, swept hundreds of demonstrators led by Indian workers. In the vanguard, saris swirling, were the Indian women. Not submissive, housebound women but Grunwick strikers – fists raised in anger. Not the inarticulate immigrant women we are often told about. Hardly. For at every building they passed they shouted their one resounding slogan: Union! Union! We want Union.

(*Black Trade Union Magazine*, Issue 197)

B The company by dismissing all the strikers, refusing to reconsider the reinstatement of any of them, refusing to seek a negotiated settlement to the strike and rejecting ACAS [Advisory, Conciliation and Arbitration Service] offers of conciliation, has acted within the letter but outside the spirit of the law. Further, such action on the part of the company was unreasonable when judged by the norms of good industrial relations practice. The company has thus added to the bitterness of the dispute, and contributed to its development into a threat of civil disorder.

(Lord Justice Scarman's report, 25 August 1977)

C The evidence relating to the experiences of young black women workers is not conclusive. Studies in Lewisham, Walsall and Leicester suggest that young black workers, both male and female, experience difficulties getting a job and that when they do it will be at a lower level than their white equivalent. Asian young women appear to have fared worst of all. There is also evidence that black workers are over represented in traditional declining industries. For example in Bradford in 1978, 66 per cent of black female school leavers obtained work in clothing and distribution compared to 41 per cent of all female school leavers. However, there is also some evidence that British born young black workers are entering higher level jobs than their parents and that they are actively encouraged by their parents to seek qualifications . . . . There is a strong tradition of union membership among black workers. However, women membership levels for white and black women are about the same (one in three). Membership is higher among West Indian women than Asian women and within the Asian groups membership is particularly low for Moslem women.

(*Women in the Labour Market: A TUC Report*, Trades Union Congress, 1983)

D Positive or affirmative action does not mean employing less qualified applicants because of their sex or race. Nor does it imply discrimination *against* men or whites. But it does commit managements and chapels to survey the firm's current employment practices for hidden barriers to equality in order to abolish them. For example:

* Do stated or implicit age limits rule out many women applicants (who may be re-entering journalism after raising a family)?

* Is experience on Fleet Street (where women and blacks are grossly underrepresented) considered essential for certain jobs?

* Do night work or overtime requirements rule out mothers of young children?

* Does your firm have any internal training programmes? Are women *encouraged* to use them?

(*Negotiating for Equality*, NUJ Equality Working Party, 1980)

Questions

1 What impression of the Grunwick strikers comes across in A? Why is this different from many people's ideas about Asian women?

2 What did Lord Justice Scarman mean by saying that the management at Grunwick 'has acted within the letter but outside the spirit of the law' (B)?

3 Why have black women taken such a low profile in trade unions?

4 What particular concerns of ethnic minority women could you expect a union to be interested in?

CHAPTER 4

Black Women and the Armed Forces

Amelia King

Amelia King was born in Stepney, East London, of West Indian parents. Her family was third generation, having lived in Britain for many years. Her father and brothers served in the merchant and royal navy. In 1943 she made application to join the service with the Women's Land Army, which took over the farm work in Britain while the men were away. She was passed over, however, rejected because she was black. She was refused her place in the war effort because some local farmers on the committee objected to her because of her colour. Other locals did not want to have her billeted with them.

The issue was raised in the House of Commons. The Minister of Agriculture was quick to make unsatisfactory excuses saying that, because of the difficulty encountered in trying to find suitable billeting accommodation for Miss King, she was advised to volunteer for some other war service.

Question

1 Amelia King felt a moral obligation as a British woman to join the war effort. What do you think was meant by the statement of the Minister of Agriculture?

Tell Me It's True

Records show that there were black people with the Roman occupation of the British Isles long before the English Angles came here. There were African soldiers among the troops stationed at Hadrian's Wall in the third century.

Black people's involvement in the defence of Britain goes back hundreds of years. In the eighteenth century black slaves were recruited into the British army and navy in the American war of independence (1775-83). In return they were offered their freedom. After the war, however, many of these war veterans found themselves starving on the streets of London, unable to find work and reduced to begging.

In the First World War eight regiments from what was then the West Indian Regiment went to serve in the fighting. On their return to Britain, conditions were very dismal as there was no work or suitable accommodation for them. Ernest Mark joined the forces during the 'Great War'. He was from Africa and, as a young man, fit and healthy, was attracted by the adventure and sense of patriotism which existed at that time among British subjects from the

15 Soldiers from the British West Indian Regiment in France, 1916

Commonwealth. Others like him would volunteer their services during the Second World War.

The year 1990 marked the 50th anniversary of the Second World War. But amidst all the pageantry, celebrations and endless reruns of war movies, there was little mention of the thousands of men and women from the Commonwealth who rallied to support Britain. These people were in no way coming as casual visitors. They stayed the full period and were relegated to assisting in the many services created to fight the war.

By 1942 there were already 10,000 black service personnel in Britain. Over the war period there would be up to ten times as many recorded in Britain to help fight the war. Most of the service people from the Caribbean volunteered – there was no such thing as compulsory conscription, though recruitment centres were established permanently in the Caribbean until 1962. Many paid their own fares to come to Britain in order to boost the war effort. They felt it their duty to defend 'democracy' and their 'mother country'.

At the start of the war the propaganda machinery was carrying messages to the Commonwealth people about contributing their services in order to strengthen the operation. Qualified and unqualified black people, whether working informally as volunteers, ancillaries, or as skilled workers and commissioned officers with the war sector, had the potential to offer practical support of a high standard. Their ability to work as a team and their commitment to the cause made them very valuable to Britain. Trinidad and Jamaica both sent entire squadrons. Some of the troops died in the Battle of Britain and have been conveniently forgotten by the host country.

Those Commonwealth citizens who could not make the journey were also prepared to do their bit for Britain. Black women knitted warm clothing. Hard wood and clothes were sent and even an ambulance was donated and shipped to Britain.

Both in terms of human resources and equipment the Caribbean, considering its size, made a determined effort to support the war in every possible way. Many black ex-service men and women are in no doubt in recognizing that the Empire came to the aid of Britain without hesitation.

But on reflection, they are of the impression that it was really just a propaganda exercise by Britain to boost numbers and establish a stronger foothold of power in the eyes of the enemy. Those who still live in Britain receive a war pension today of £6.48 per week, not a lot for putting your life on the front line. The black war widows and the disabled veterans were just signed off and forgotten.

Ivan Mendez, an ex-service man himself and a historian, is keen to bring into the open the hypocrisies that have existed for the past 50 years and are kept hidden by the British government. He suggests that:

The government is just being two-faced. When it suits them and they need us, they're quite content to use us. But when it comes to getting the credit . . . .
(*The Voice*, 9 January 1990)

Black service personnel found their reception in Britain a strange cocktail of genuine welcome and direct discrimination. Prejudice was often encouraged by the white troops. Black troops were harassed on the streets and thrown out of dance halls, restaurants and public places where they went to enjoy themselves. These service people and skilled workers were rightly hurt and disillusioned by the racial discrimination they encountered in Britain.

16 ATS recruits from the Caribbean, 1943

Many black women, like Amelia King, were denied entry to the WLA. Others were accepted to the Auxiliary Territorial Service (ATS) but experienced discrimination there. An article in the journal *John Bull* (26 January 1946) gave examples of insulting behaviour experienced by black women in the ATS.

A West Indian girl in the ATS was refused a new issue of shoes by her officer, who added, 'At home you don't wear shoes anyway'. Another Army Officer said to a West Indian ATS 'If I can't get white women I'll something well do without'.

Young black women who join the services today experience much frustration and feel demoralized. They are deprived of any information about black people in the war. Sharon, a black woman of 24, views her promotion prospects within the army as being very slim.

Many black women are ignorant of the major contribution made by their grandparents. There is very little acknowledgement of it in history books and the museums are largely devoid of reminders of the part played by black people in Britain's wars.

A number of black people join the armed services

today, although figures show that they are not attracting the same percentage as in the 1970s. Peat Marwick McLintock found in his report *Ethnic Minority Recruitment to the Armed Services* (Ministry of Defence, 1990) that only eight per cent of Asians and 9 per cent of Afro-Caribbeans have seriously considered a career in the services, compared with 19 per cent of whites.

Evidence

A The 1981 recruiting brochure from the Queen Alexandra's Royal Army Nursing Corps shows a photograph of eight 'QA' nurses. Seven of the eight smiling British women are white, each dressed in the uniform of a different nursing rank. But the Ministry of Defence's advertising specialists added an eighth woman: an Asian British nurse. She represents a lower-ranking nurse. Nowhere else in the brochure, which entices potential women enlistees with pictures of the varied duties of today's military nurse, is another Asian or black nurse (or soldier) shown . . . . Despite the nods toward a multi-racial image by military recruitment advertisers, Britain's military nursing corps and the government civilian nursing sector look quite different in racial mix in the 1980s. National Health Service nurses and hospital workers are drawn heavily from Asian and West Indian immigrants and from the growing population of black and Asian women born in Britain. The same does not hold for military nursing.
(Cynthia Enloe, *Does Khaki Become You? The Militarization of Women's Lives*, Pandora Press 1988)

B . . . fear of racial discrimination is one of the main reasons why ethnic minorities do not apply to the Services. This appears to be a reflex reaction and is based largely on impressions gained from the media. When young people consider the issue further, the possibility of encountering racial discrimination in work generally is not seen as very different from expectations of discrimination in the Services.
(Peat Marwick McLintock, *Ethnic Minority Recruitment to the Armed Services*, Ministry of Defence, 1990)

C It's still very traditional in the Armed Forces . . . . You want the status . . . the nice jobs never come our way, if they do they don't go to black women.
(Tracey Morris, Women's Territorial Unit)

D Being a woman and black doesn't help matters . . . .
(ex-Hendon Police School Cadet)

Questions

1 In A, what comparison is drawn between nurses in the armed forces and those in the National Health Service? Do you think this is the fault of advertising?

2 Why do you think young people from ethnic minorities feel that racial discrimination in the armed services is particularly bad? Do you agree with what is said in B?

3 A number of black Second World War veterans are still alive and now elderly. Why has the British government failed to recognize their contribution?

4 Why do you think it is so difficult to get facts about the history and way of life of black people?

CHAPTER 5

Black Women and the Health Service

Cherry Byfield (b. 15 January 1939)

Cherry Byfield is a black woman who came to Britain to train as a nurse in the 1960s. Her decision to come to Britain was a result of the death of her husband. She left behind her young baby with her mother, who was keen to support her daughter and dedicate her time to raising her grandson in Jamaica.

She came to a hospital in north Manchester in October 1961 to begin her three-year training. She had the intention of doing her training, earning some money and returning to the West Indies after five years in Britain.

She vividly remembers how Britain was described to her as a place which was cold from eight o'clock in the morning till five at night, not at all like Jamaica. On her arrival she was confronted with many new experiences as she attempted to settle in and find her way around the system. As she recalls, 'It was warmer to be in bed than anywhere else, it was so cold'.

The winter of 1961 happened to be very cold with temperatures plummeting well below zero. This cold climate was reflected in the government's policies towards immigration. In the 1960s Enoch Powell came to prominence as the Tory Minister for Health. He became actively involved in the recruitment of black labour from the Commonwealth and welcomed black nurses to Britain. He had a change of heart and in 1968 made speeches prophesying 'rivers of blood' if black immigration continued. He encouraged racial hatred by predicting industrial downfall as well as calling for black people to leave Britain and return to their own countries. This was the political climate into which Cherry came.

Cherry's first contact with senior nursing staff was not a very pleasant one. The matron of the hospital wanted to relegate Cherry to the SEN (state enrolled nurse) training. At this first meeting the matron had already made her decision about this black woman who wanted to train as an SRN (state registered nurse). (SRNs are more highly qualified than SENs). Cherry

17 *Cherry Byfield*

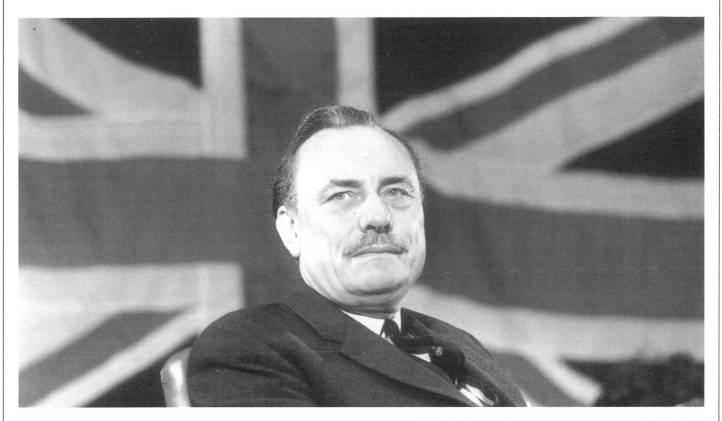

17a Enoch Powell – who as Minister for Health supported the recruitment of black workers from the Caribbean

stood her ground and defended her position. She was instructed that she would have to take a written examination. She was also questioned about her background, status and possible prospects of having children while on the course. Finally, after much disagreement, she was allowed to pursue her chosen area of training.

Cherry can remember being given highly unpleasant menial tasks to do which other black nurses also experienced. The long hours which nurses had to work meant that many of their meals were taken while at work. It was quite normal for the working day to begin at 7.30 am and go straight through until 4.30 pm. Both patients and staff alike could be very unkind, demanding and insulting.

Sometimes the wards were short of staff so meal times passed by and a quick snack would have to be taken whenever a quiet moment occurred. Black nurses would bring in a packed meal to eat whenever they had a break, as the meals in the staff canteen were not always appealing. Cherry recalls an incident when a nurse entered the rest room where she and other black colleagues were tucking into their snack. The

nurse asked, 'What's that your eating? It looks like hog food'. It was actually an interesting combination of vegetables and fish. Cherry and her friends did not feel able to respond assertively for fear of the horrible jobs they would be made to carry out, as well as being reported to the deputy matron when she made her rounds. There was an atmosphere of high anxiety among black nurses in the hospital. They felt exploited and that prejudice from other staff was being directed at them.

Cherry completed her nurse training despite the cultural differences and the obstacles she had to face. She remained in student nurses's uniform for many months before being allowed to wear the staff outfit.

Having passed through the ranks she chose to apply for a senior sister's position. A deputy sister's post was offered instead, in a psychiatry unit.

Cherry took the job, but several weeks later the matron telephoned to tell her to go to the sewing room to be measured up for the senior sister's uniform. Had there been any evident competition Cherry would not have minded having had to wait so long for the post, but there was no one to challenge her position. The only thing delaying her promotion was the matron. The matron did not congratulate Cherry or acknowledge that she was the best person for the post.

18 A senior nursing officer and a radiologist in a premature baby unit

As a senior sister, she again came up against the prejudices of white health workers – this time doctors, who challenged her managerial abilities in front of other white professionals. At an important meeting with staff drawn from many disciplines, a senior doctor remarked,

'I think that you should nurse your own people in your own environment and social group'.

Cherry went on to become a senior nurse manager as well as a magistrate and active community worker in the city of Manchester. She has since taken early retirement and returned to the West Indies. Despite the set backs, she feels very positive about the steady wind of change which is taking place in our society.

Questions

1 Enoch Powell was responsible for encouraging nurses to come to Britain to train and work but later wanted to stop immigration. What do you think he meant by 'rivers of blood' occurring if immigration continued? What effect do you think his speeches had on the existing black community in Britain?

2 What do you think would have happened to Cherry if she had resisted the unpleasant tasks she was given to do in a confused way?

3 Cherry remains optimistic about the future of black health workers in Britain. In what ways do you think she feels optimistic and why?

It's Only a Job of Work

There have been many important figures in the history of black nursing. Mary Seacole is one of them. She was widely renowned in her own time, but forgotten again until the 1980s. Mary Seacole was a Jamaican nurse who was born in 1805 in Kingston of mixed race parents. Her father was a Scottish soldier and her mother was a practitioner of traditional Jamaican medicine. She was brought up in a boarding house which her mother ran for wounded British officers. Mary Seacole developed a reputation for being a skilful nurse and healer. She travelled widely, offering her expertise everywhere she went.

Mary Seacole was aware of the desperate situation of the British army in the Crimean war and made a formal application to the war departments offering excellent testimonials from the officers she had cared for. She was refused entry. Despite this drawback, she used her own money to buy medicines, bandages, food and other essential equipment and made the journey as a

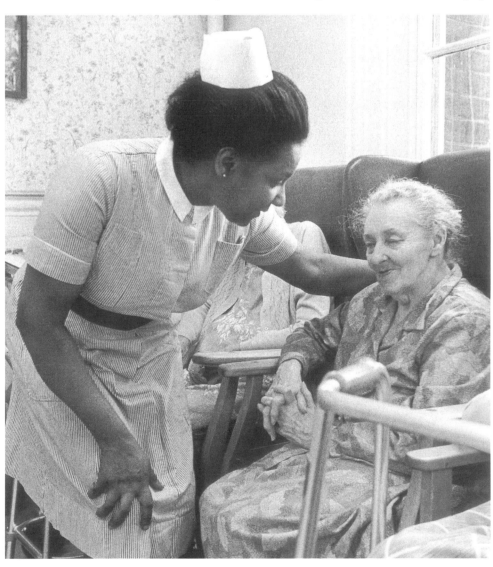

19 Often black health workers have felt that they have been pushed into 'low status' areas such as geriatrics

sutler (one who follows an army selling provisions to troops). She opened up a hotel between Balaklava and Sebastopol which would become a store, dispensary and hospital. Her nursing skills gained her wide recognition and acceptance.

Ms Seacole experienced bankruptcy as the war came to an end and she was forced to return to Britain where she lived in poverty and ill health. In recognition of her services to the war, two commanders of the British army held a fund-raising event for her benefit. At an official dinner, she was cheered and saluted by 'adoring soldiers'. She was awarded a Crimean medal but was never given the adulation which Florence Nightingale received for her contribution to nursing. She eventually passed into obscurity and died in Britain. She was buried in a London cemetery and every year a memorial service is held to remember her work and contribution.

With the creation of the National Health Service in 1948, there was a greater demand for hospitals and medical services to be staffed by fit and healthy white workers. But with the shortage of labour after the Second World War large numbers of black women were recruited to fill gaps in the public sector, primarily in the hospitals as nurses, cleaners, cooks and orderlies.

The health service was in no way geared up to receive black people as clients; they were coming to work. The Health Service has to be shaped by financial and administrative considerations, rather than being planned solely around community needs. Part of the plan, back in the early 1950s, was to attract black people from the Commonwealth to provide cheap labour and enable the service to run efficiently. This cost effectiveness was achieved at the expense of the stress caused by long hours and the health hazards that black women in the NHS had to undergo.

Nowhere have women been more welcomed than in the many fields of the health service where their services as semi-skilled and unskilled workers could support the fabric of the NHS. Because of the labour shortages, the NHS was exempted from the restrictions of the Immigration Acts of 1962 and 1965. Many of the black women that came to work in the NHS did not want to work in unskilled jobs but wanted to train as nurses. British nursing schools generally asked for much higher academic qualification from overseas nurses wishing to train as Registered nurses.

I came over from Jamaica in the 70s to train as an SRN, with three 'A' levels. I realised when I started the course that it was only the overseas trainee nurses that had 'A' levels.
(Staff Nurse Wilmott, London Hospital)

Some of the girls in my intake had 'O' levels but most only had CSEs.
(Afro-Caribbean nurse, 1990)

In the early 1970s many of the nurses were directed into State Enrolled Nurse training. In 1972 figures showed that the number of NHS nurses from overseas amounted to nine per cent. But they made up 20 per cent of the total number of SENs working in the NHS. Often nurses were not told until long after starting their course that there was a difference between the two qualifications. By then it was too late to change courses. The SEN was not recognized outside Britain and so was of no practical use for those black women who wanted to return home after their training.

With increasing unemployment, the situation has become worse. There is now no recruitment of overseas nurses as in 1983 work permits were withdrawn, thus denying overseas nurses entry to Britain. Some Schools of nursing have developed policies which discriminate against black school leavers in a number of ways. Entry requirements have become far higher than required by the General Nursing Council (GNC). Once in training, ethnic minority nurses are often encouraged to specialize in low status areas such as geriatrics and mental illness. According to GNC figures, one-third of overseas learners are in psychiatric and mental handicap nursing. Furthermore, many young black girls are not prepared to put up with the discrimination and unequal treatment their mothers experienced whilst training to be nurses.

When I was being trained, the black nurses were sent to do the geriatrics option and the white ones to do obstetrics or the community option.
(Mental Health nurse from Mauritius)

Health visitors from the ethnic minorities are particularly underrepresented. To be successful, health visitor training depends on a sound academic background and broad vocational experience in the field of nurse care. Some Health Authorities are aware of the importance of reviewing their recruiting policies, which should take into consideration appropriate experience rather than formal qualifications. Despite this action, many ethnic minority nurses are still being excluded from health visitor training and prevented from working within multiracial communities which would greatly benefit from their common black experience. One black candidate for a health visitor course said: 'I was asked at one point during the interview, "Some white families might object to a coloured health visitor. How do you feel about that?"'

Over a third of all the hospitals in the UK employ doctors from overseas. The number of black women doctors remains a very small percentage. They face discrimination and, like black nurses, tend to be given posts in the least well-equipped hospitals and departments, such as geriatrics and mental health.

Doctor Khan, who came to Britain from India at the age of eight, is now a doctor in a London hospital. She says:

> I think the patients are shocked when they first see me, and think, is she as good as the white doctor . . . I've undergone the same intensive training and have the experience . . . I'm concerned about their health and they're a person to me irrespective of the colour difference between us.

Evidence

A A prestigious London nursing school is reviewing its staff recruitment procedures after an industrial tribunal ruled a black applicant for a tutor's job was the victim of racial discrimination.

The nurse, Daphne McKenzie, had been a clinical teacher and a nurse for 29 years before she went on a tutor's course, hoping to get a job at the Nightingale school at St Thomas' hospital. She did not get the job and an industrial tribunal has ruled that questions asked at her interview were irrelevant to her ability to fulfil the demands of the post.
(*Nursing Times*, 4 February 1987)

B I remember when I was appointed as senior sister, this caused much apprehension. One consultant doctor, in particular, vetted every move I made. Once during a ward round he remarked, 'I think these girls should be nursing their own people of the same social and cultural backgrounds in their own environment'.

When I got the job, the reaction from the rest of the staff was very disturbing. There were numerous insults and unpleasant remarks. I felt isolated. Nurses and auxiliaries refused to work under me. Senior staff disarranged my ward programme in my absence so as to cause confusion in ward policy and embarrassment to my administration. I was told by the staff nurse that, if sufficient pressure was brought to bear on me, I would have to run away from the job.
(Black senior sister, quoted in Carol Baxter, *The Black Nurse: An Endangered Species*), Training in Health and Race, 1988)

C The most extreme example of a black nurse being victimised for this reason occurred in a North London hospital to a Trinidadian student nurse, here on a student visa. This nurse wore her hair in a plait, away from her face and off her shoulders. For some time a nursing sister had been quite rude and had been giving this nurse hell on the ward – aways telling her that nothing she did was correct, making racist remarks about her hair style to both senior and junior white nurses on the ward. Finally, the sister could not contain herself any longer and she told the nurse to change her hair style and wear it like the other 'Afro' black nurses on the ward who, apart from one, had their hair straightened and styled in a European fashion. The nurse refused to undo her plait and the principal nursing officer was called. When she came to the ward, she demanded that the nurse undo her hair, warning her that if she did not her nursing training would be in jeopardy – she was working on a student visa which had to be renewed six-monthly, on the recommendation of her employer (i.e. the hospital). The principal nursing officer implied that she would be on the next plane to Trinidad if she did not do as she was told. Humiliated in front of the patients on the ward and her fellow nursing colleagues, the student nurse undid her plait.
('A Black Nurse Speaks Out (St Ann's Hospital)', *Black Health Workers and Patients Group Bulletin*, No. 1)

D An unqualified white nurse stood over us and told us to go into the slouch and wash out wooden commodes. We had to do this without any gloves or disinfectant. My friend got sick of this and refused to do it. There was a lot of heated discussion, but we stood our ground.
(Peggy Roberts, SEN, 1960s)

E Promotion for black nurses is only ever available in low status disciplines such as mental health nursing. It is very rare that you find a black nurse running or even staffing on surgical wards. This seems to be reserved for whites.
(Afro-Caribbean nurse, 1989)

Questions

1 In A, why was Daphne McKenzie the victim of racial discrimination? What questions do you think she was asked at her interview? What questions should she have been asked?

2 In all of these sources, what common experiences do these nurses share?

3 In the 1960s, discrimination was shown by personal dislike and uneasiness in the presence of black nurses. What evidence is there to suggest that black health workers were being discriminated against?

4 We hear and read a lot about Florence Nightingale and the work she did during the Crimean War. Can you suggest why the same recognition was not given to Mary Seacole?

CHAPTER 6

Black Women in the Community

Barbara Carter (b. 14 December 1914)

Barbara Carter arrived in Britain in September 1939, married and with a baby daughter in her arms. Her husband had been working in Paris and then moved on to Belgium. With the start of the Second World War, the British Consulate in Belgium advised the Carter family to return to Britain. They arrived at Victoria Station in London and proceeded to hail a taxi and find suitable accommodation. They tried several hotels but were told they were full. Finally they arrived at a hotel in Russell Square. The commissioner at the doors informed them that there were no vacancies. As the taxi moved off, they heard him say, 'We don't have niggers here'.

They eventually found a hotel room in Victoria and were able to settle in and get over the shocking experience they had just undergone. They soon found a small flat in north London. The war had started and Barbara's husband offered his services to the Royal Air Force. He was not signed up and chose not to be humiliated again by reapplying. When he was finally called up he was able to get exemption and, instead, entertained the troops at the different camps around Britain. Barbara was conscripted but, as she had a very young child, she was not drafted in to do heavy work. She volunteered to work in the nurseries and was accepted. They moved to a bigger flat in Baker Street. Barbara now had two young children.

Her husband's war service took him to many camps, where he met other black men and women serving in the British army. He would often invite them home. Barbara would cook and offer warm hospitality to the many black service personnel who came to visit and

20 Barbara Carter

21 *A small black boy among a group of evacuees from London in 1940*

shelter by Barbara and her children would bring her white neighbours' helping hands forward to carry and support her children and bags and make room for them. Her presence was also seen as a good luck symbol.

Food was rationed during the war. Shopkeepers were generous to Barbara and helped out in whatever way they were able. Extra fruit, the odd egg or bit of margarine was added to her rations.

Bombing continued and was particularly bad in the centre of London where Barbara lived. The family decided to move out of London and took the initiative to travel to Wales, paying their own fare and intending to seek out suitable accommodation. This took some time and they eventually had to take an attic room. The very night they left their flat in London the area received a direct hit by a bomb and was flattened. Residents in the immediate and surrounding vicinity were killed. Barbara recalls, 'Oh, it was terrible. It was just as well we got away from Baker Street . . . it was really chaos'.

After the birth of her third child, which was delivered at Ruskin College, transformed into a maternity hospital, Barbara returned to London. She struggled on and managed with her three young children. The 'open door' was still there for anyone who wanted to feel at home, eat some good food and meet other black entertainers, academics and service people. Everyone who went to her home remembered those days fondly. Rita Kahn, a cabaret singer in the 1940s, said, 'Some of the great black entertainers would meet at her home'. Singer Lauretta Johnson said of Barbara, 'She had a generous heart . . . her door was always open'. Some men and women who met at Barbara's house during those war days got together, got engaged and eventually married. They continue to this day to keep in contact and visit her whenever they can.

Barbara Carter has spent 51 years in Britain, more than half of her life. She takes pride in her own strength and independence. She never hesitated to offer support and companionship to the many black people who came to her house during those turbulent days. She is in her seventies now with grown-up children and grandchildren. Her home in West London still rings with laughter and an open-door hospitality is maintained for anyone who is passing through. She spends half the year in Canada with her relatives and the other in Britain.

share good times together. One RAF serviceman from the West Indies said: 'Our main source of socializing was visiting each other. Babs' home was one of the principal meeting places. Many would give her name to the Red Cross when they had to go into active service. They had a nickname for her, the 'Black Ambassadoress'. She received many telegrams telling of her friends' deaths and injuries in action.

In the war, community spirit was particularly warm and caring between black and white in a way that it hadn't been before. A necessary visit to an air raid

22 *A Caribbean club in the late 1940s*

Questions

1 Why do you think that during the war years the main way of socializing for black people was 'visiting each other'?

2 Why was Barbara Carter's presence in the air raid shelter seen as a symbol of good luck? Do we make other associations like this one?

Letting Them Know We Are Here

Women all over the world have learnt and handed down the deeply felt duty and role of being a mother, wife, woman and helper to those in need. The different ways of doing things of a community depend on its make-up and needs. No two British families are the same but certain values and assumptions in common form the majority British cultural and social norms. These influence the way that administrators and others identify what services and facilities communities require. There has been a tendency therefore for decisions to reflect 'majority' culture (i.e. 'white') values.

These decisions have not always taken into account the multiracial needs and rights of our communities.

Some people still feel that ethnic minority communities must adapt to the services offered in Britain or do without. If services provided for the community are organized, intentionally or unintentionally, to discriminate against people because their way of life is different from the majority, then communities take it upon themselves to change this. Many of our multiracial communities live in socially deprived inner city areas and experience all the problems that go with that.

Most black people who came to Britain settled in the West Midlands, the North West and the South East. These were the areas of labour shortage and contain the largest proportion of what are considered inner city areas.

Cities like Bristol, Manchester, Liverpool, Cardiff and London have attracted some of Britain's longest established black communities. Decision makers in

these cities have long assumed that the longer black people live in Britain, then the more likely they are to integrate and become better accepted by the host country. Black people have lived in Liverpool for over 300 years but the level of discrimination and racial harassment has not got better. In fact, it remains extremely high compared with other places, like Birmingham, Manchester and London.

There are some black Liverpudlians who can trace their ancestors back to 1753. At their height the Liverpool docks where handling up to 95 per cent of the slave trade and during the period of the colonialist era up to 82 per cent of the world's shipping passed through Liverpool. The African and Afro-Caribbean seamen married white women and the first racial mix in Britain developed.

Black immigration also came to Britain through other routes, during the two world wars and then in the post-war era. The black American, Asian and Afro-Caribbean immigrants made their homes in cities

22a The Calabash – a day centre for the elderly in Lewisham

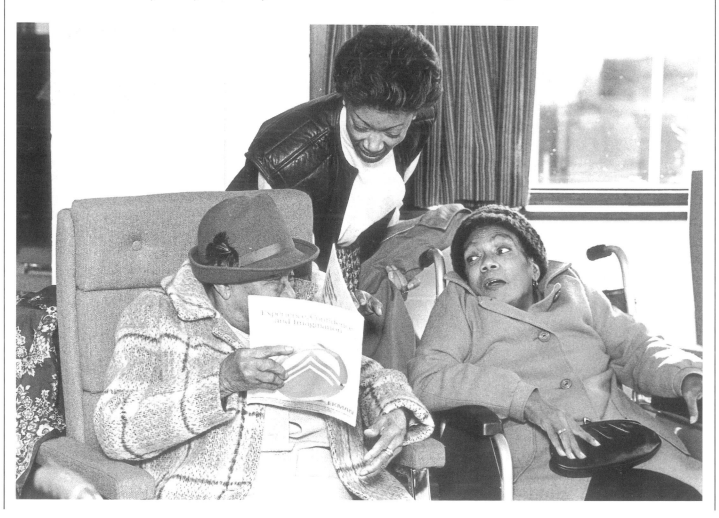

23 Religion plays an important part in community life

where ethnic minorities had already laid down their roots. Some people chose to live in inner city areas because:

- people of the same culture lived close by

- there were delicatessen and ethnic shops in the area

- their place of worship could easily be reached

- there was a sense of security offered by numbers.

Quite recent research by a sociologist C. Brown shows that white people in Britain vary hugely in their knowledge of how many of their fellow citizens are black. A survey of the replies of young people to the question showed a wide difference in estimates. For instance, Susan Thomas, a teenager from Newport in Wales, thought that less than two per cent of the population was black. But in Leicester, Maxine Skervin thought 50 per cent of the population was black or Asian. The true answer, had Susan and Maxine known it, was that just over six per cent of the population in Britain is, in official language, 'non-white'. In mid-Wales a black face is quite rare, but in Leicester, in the Midlands, Maxine felt she was surrounded by black faces. People who live in the big cities tend to overestimate the number of black and Asian people who have settled in Britain.

Attitudes to black people and Asians are often affected by whether an area has them as part of their community. There appears to be less discrimination in areas where they live than in areas where they do not. Despite these impressions, many people still feel threatened by what they see as an overwhelming number of black faces all around them in their locality.

In areas where large numbers of immigrants settled, members of the host community who lived close by felt threatened. They could be very hostile and express their race hatred through violence and oppression. Black and Asian groups, like the Jews and Italians who came before them, have decided to confront this by

45

23a The extended family has always played an important role

drawing together. This emotional strength and support which relations and community can provide helps to reinforce the community solidarity. As one elderly black woman said, 'We cannot afford to move from here . . . if you went from here you don't know who you can rely on.'

Living with people whose culture, customs and language you are familiar with means that it is easier to live out your life in relative peace of mind and dignity.

Despite educational and social barriers, there are black people who hold down middle-class and professional occupations and have lifestyles and aspirations which are not unlike their white middle-class counterparts. Many choose to remain in their ethnic community and to offer support and voluntary work within it. Supplementary schools for children of all ages held on a Saturday are to be found in many areas, in which the teachers are black and children highly motivated under the right conditions. Religious classes and cultural activities are held weekly in the community hall or place of worship. These activities

offer something for everyone and are intended to sustain and promote the community's culture, customs and language.

Childcare facilities with a multicultural emphasis have been set up. The ethnic elderly, instead of being admitted to old people's homes, are given the right to remain in their communities and be looked after by family and the wider group. Also on a community level, individuals become involved in political activity, bringing greater awareness to all and helping to effect change and better provision of services. White volunteers often see work in these areas as less prestigious than in the more affluent parts of towns and cities. The result is that funding is not so readily available for community initiatives; services remain inadequate and inappropriate for the growing communities.

The communities do not enjoy these disadvantages and are struggling all the time to improve their social position and influence local authority policies. Back in the 1960s it was in these communities that the 'Black Movement' in Britain was formed.

Liverpool's black community has the same problems as other black communities. Since 1753 black people have only moved about two miles from the docks. Most live in the Liverpool 8 district, or what is known as Toxteth. Communities have had to fend for themselves.

> If you see a black person walking in town you say 'hello'. We regard each other as allies and help each other as much as we can.
> (Mixed-race woman, 1990)

West Indian women have always had boundless enthusiasm and commitment in contributing to their community. The church often played a very significant role in their lives and still does today. Black women account for some 60 per cent of the congregation. Church not only provided a forum for religious worship but was also a place where the welfare of others was looked after. Most of the social events such as outings, dances and meetings were organized by the women as well as refreshments, preparation of traditional dishes and childcare facilities.

In Britain, West Indian and Asian women support one another as they would have done in their own countries. Arrangements are made to take and collect children from school; they cook food for each other if they happen to be working on shift work; they pop in to each other's homes to check on children who may have to be left on their own while the women work late at night. In the 1950s and 1960s, hairdressing parlours were set up in the front rooms of people's homes. Black women would not only meet for the purpose of getting their hair straightened or pressed but used the opportunity to have informal and newsy conversations about their life, children, men and work. This weekly or monthly event became an important part of their network system.

Black women were quite used to carrying on traditional community roles which they had carried out prior to coming to Britain. Self-help groups emerged within communities. Groups of black women would get together and save on a regular basis. One person would be responsible for collecting and handing over a large sum of money every week to each group member in turn.

The money was used to help to pay for the more expensive items like a down payment on a house or the plane fare for a woman's child to come and join her in Britain. In was a real bonus known as a 'Pardner' and it still goes on as an inhouse savings scheme used by many West Indian communities. The black community is self-reliant in many cases and feels bound by a cause of self-organization and interdependence to try to move themselves ahead.

Evidence

A At home the family structure is very different. You have your mother and father, who may have their mother and father living in the same house or close by. Grandparents take a big interest in grandchildren, sometimes even looking after them. Here things are different, because families are scattered around. The family involvement in the West Indies is very tight and totally different from the family involvement here.
(Afro-Caribbean senior citizen)

B . . . the formation of the West Indian Women's Association (WIWA) in Harlesden. This initiative came from a woman who had been active in workplace activity for fifteen years . . . but she believed that the most pressing issues for the West Indian community, particularly women, were community-, not work-based issues. In addition, she had experience of working within West Indian voluntary organisations where women had been denied the opportunity of taking any real initiative. The WIWA has established practical schemes, such as supplementary education classes, has fought for better child-care facilities and in some cases set up their own schemes. The association has made a very rapid local impact.
(Annie Phizacklea, 'Migrant women and wage labour: the case of West Indian women in Britain', in Jackie West (ed.), *Work, Women and the Labour Market*, Routledge & Kegan Paul, 1982)

C There were a number of voluntary organisations in the area where I lived. The one that stands out most in my mind is an organisation which, as one of its many roles, campaigned and raised funds for 'Summer Play Schemes' for children in the locality. Due to the success of the Play Schemes, the organisation soon extended itself to providing a 'Supplementary School' aimed at Afro-Caribbean and Asian children, where they could be tutored in those subjects in which they lacked confidence. Of equal importance, however, the role of the Supplementary School was to counteract Eurocentric state education, by providing a cultural input into the education of those who attended.

My initial involvement in both the Summer Play Scheme and the Supplementary School was very basic, but at the time it seemed very exciting. During those years my perception of things was very localised, and it was not until some time later that I realised that Black people in many different parts of the country had set up, and were setting up, similar organisations. To be realistic, it is obvious that there is an immediate need for us as Black people to create these types of organisations for ourselves: not only to fill the huge gaps in our education, but to provide positive images and some motivation for ourselves. However, there is now a part of me that realises the double-sided effect of this, because as long as we continue to 'provide for ourselves' the state conveniently fails to recognise the lack in its own provision.

(Agnes Quashie, 'Coming of Age' in Joan Scanlon (ed.), *Surviving the Blues: Growing up in the Thatcher Decade*, Virago, 1990)

Questions

1 What differences did women find between communities in the Caribbean and in Britain?

2 How have black women responded to the lack of state-provided amenities? Are they happy to do this?

3 What do you think attracted immigrants to the big cities in the 1960s and 1970s? What are the benefits and what are the disadvantages of inner-city life?

4 For over half a century large numbers of black people have lived and worked in Britain, contributing to the economy. They have often been blamed when 'things go wrong'. What kind of things have gone wrong? Are black people to blame?

Black Women Who Talk Writing

Lauretta Ngcobo (b. 13 September 1930)

One of the cornerstones of black women writers in Britain today is the South African writer Lauretta Ngcobo. She speaks of herself as being a writer in exile, which suggests that her roots and life have been displaced.

South Africa operates a system of separating black and white people. This is called 'apartheid'. The minority whites hold economic and political power. The black people have been fighting for majority rule since the 1950s. Lauretta was born in South Africa where she grew up and attended a famous missionary institution run by the Americans. She went to university, trained as a teacher and got married to a fellow South African.

When in the early 1960s she began teaching in a secondary school, the political climate of South Africa was very extreme and oppressive. Lauretta became interested in politics when she was a university undergraduate. Later on she became politically active in a way which gave her and many of her people an opportunity to work alongside the African National Congress (ANC), the main African freedom movement, and take up interests which deeply concerned them. They also had misgivings and were suspicious about the way the movement was developing and handling their interests.

In the 1950s, many of the white Communists who had been ousted from the South African National party found a place in the ANC. They began to take a high profile in the movement and directed the nature of the black people's struggle in south Africa. This created a lot of resentment among the black members who were rightly angered and offended by the takeover.

Throughout the fifties, this fight continued within the ANC. It finally culminated in 1958 with a section of the movement breaking away and forming themselves into a group called the Pan African Congress. Lauretta's husband was a member of this

24 *Lauretta Ngcobo*

breakaway faction along with other famous South African activists.

The ideas of Pan Africanism are about taking steps to influence change, policies and public opinion on issues which directly affect the wellbeing and existence of people in various parts of the world, like South and West Africa, the West Indies and America. It is based on the concept that black people all over the world are Africans.

Many members of the Pan African movement were arrested and placed in prison. Lauretta's husband was one of these. First he was detained, then charged and finally imprisoned for three years in a prison some 500 miles away in Pretoria. It was during this time, while he was in prison and Lauretta was teaching, that the young people that she taught began to ask questions and probe her about the political activity which was surging through the country at the time.

They saw Lauretta as a focal point, as they knew her husband was imprisoned for his activities. Their questions were endless and revealed to Lauretta how little information they had access to. Because of press restrictions and censorship, people were very ignorant of what was happening in their own country and in the rest of the world. She took it upon herself to help them along, open up their thinking and show them that a world existed. She devised ways to communicate with her students in a fairly open manner through discussion, debates and short talks, using the materials she had to broaden their awareness and make them better-informed citizens.

Despite the penalties, she was not afraid. In Lauretta's words, 'To fight a struggle you derive the energy from the people'.

Lauretta realized that she was being very political in her approach. Her students were responding to this by their behaviour in their communities and direct clashes with the police. The government was becoming very restless and reacted by intimidating the young people. Lauretta received warnings from the parents of her children that the police knew about her political activity in the schools and were out to get her.

In 1963 the state of affairs was devastating. Schools were swamped by the police who swept away numbers of young black people and put them into prison. Some even died for the cause. Somewhere, somehow the police would find an incriminating piece of evidence in their personal belongings and use this to charge them.

Lauretta felt it her duty to help those who had not yet come under the political chopper to escape as quickly as possible. Her life was in danger but as luck would have it she got knowledge that the police were coming to arrest her and was able to escape. She shares her thoughts at the time:

> The next morning I was trying to make up my mind what to do. My husband was still in prison. My children were very young. I decided at first I would just wait and go to prison but later on I argued with myself. I had helped everybody to escape and I decided to leave that evening. I left. At 5.00 am that morning they came to pick me up. I went into exile.

She went to Swaziland were she remained with her children for two years. During that time her husband was released from prison and was able to visit the family. He had to pass on to other black Africans the notions of Pan Africanism and try to keep the movement alive outside South Africa. They moved to Zambia where Lauretta continued her career as a teacher. Five years later the family moved to Britain as a result of her husband coming to study. This also gave Lauretta the opportunity to have her family together after many years of being separated from one another. As a family they had never lived together for longer than 18 months.

She recalls:

> We would come and live with him as a family for the first time, he was studying here. It was the only opportunity for my husband to see the children. Our daughter of five he had never seen before because when he visited me in Swaziland it was without the children. This was the sort of marriage we had.

In September 1969 Lauretta and her family arrived in Britain. She dreaded coming to Britain as historical and personal experiences had shown her that being ruled by a white society meant pain, oppression, injustice and maybe even death. Would it be like living in South Africa all over again?

Lauretta's first book was written as the result of the fear and disillusionment which preoccupied her mind. She was convinced that she had made a terrible mistake in coming to Britain. In her novel, *Cross of Gold*, she was trying to retrace her steps to find out whether or not she had choices. Could she have made alternative moves? Using her main character, a black woman in South Africa, Lauretta explores women's role in the struggle. The character dies but her son takes her place. Lauretta wrote to explore her inner self and her history.

The family lived in London and Lauretta decided not to go immediately into teaching but instead trained in office technology. When she took a job in an office, she did not enjoy it and very soon returned to teaching in the primary school sector. She found the environment terribly alien and the children boisterous and uncontrollable. Almost 18 months later she found herself observing a situation between a new teacher and those same children. They reacted to the new teacher just as they had reacted to her when she first started, but the new teacher was white. When they later met the teacher confessed that she could not teach the children because they were so naughty and disruptive. Lauretta immediately realized that it was not the colour of her skin which had caused the children to behave the way they did, it was simply that 'they were horrible, and they were naughty'.

From that day she regained her confidence and head held high, she determined to do her job to the best of her ability. The children accepted her position as the authority in the classroom and the atmosphere changed to be a cooperative and productive one. She retrained as an infant teacher and was promoted to be a deputy headteacher.

In 1983 she was offered the post of headteacher of a primary school in South London. She refused the post because it was around this time that she was beginning to immerse herself in her writing. She had been published and was in demand. At the same time as being recognized and accepted within literary circles, she was being asked to attend conferences, write articles and academic papers. All these things were dazzling, new and exciting and took up a lot of Lauretta's time. She was commissioned to edit a book about black women's writing in Britain, *Let it be Told*.

In this book, she brings together several writers and tackles issues which are controversial and which she feels have not been picked up and understood fully by young black women readers. Nevertheless, she has received a lot of attention from people in academic circles and praise from black people everywhere.

In her introduction to the book, she writes:

> Published writings by Black women in Britain are still relatively few and far between. We do not apologize for this. Black British society as a viable entity is very young indeed, barely 50 years old . . . .

As soon as she finished this project she started on her third book, *And They Didn't Die*, published in 1990. The novel is about black women in South Africa and draws on the happy experiences Lauretta had as a child being brought up by these special and powerful women. She reflects some of this in the book but still feels that she has not done them the justice they deserve.

She has since retired from being a headteacher but continues to write papers and critical commentaries on different issues. She now has the opportunity to write for television as well as a book for children.

Lauretta feels very strongly that good literature which we can pass on to our children should first be given the critical treatment in an open and honest way. She believes that for black women writers to succeed they need to view their work not from the popular view point but from a literary one, putting themselves in a position to write without restriction or conforming to a particular doctrine. Only then is she sure that writers like herself, with a strong, creative, individual approach will be considered fresh, exhilarating and meaningful to those generations of young people to come.

Questions

1 What themes did Lauretta Ngcobo choose for her writing? Are these themes of interest to black women living in Britain?

2 Why can writing about experiences and events be a useful learning opportunity for others in future years?

3 What reasons does Lauretta give for the fact that there are very few published writings by black women in Britain? What other reasons do you think there might be?

A Writer Because . . . .

Know how they love to divide us
Ethnic minority of brown yellow and black
I cannot speak for all women
But worldwide I know we're in the majority
Because I too am Black

(From 'Poem for Fiona' by Fiona Walker)

Traditionally, black women have passed down stories in the oral way from grandmother to mother to daughter over the generations. Centuries ago stories were never written down. Books by black women writers today reflect something of that tradition and black history.

The well-known English classics are often prescribed reading in schools. This should never stop us from liberating ourselves and reading other books which cover a wide range of subjects. There is a tendency to do what is traditional and ignore other forms of literature. For recent generations of children, writers like Enid Blyton, Roald Dahl and Nina Bawden have been popular. But there are also writers like Petronella Breinburg or Jocelyn Maxime who write children's books with a multiracial theme.

These books have their place. Perhaps there has been some cultural conspiracy to keep educated and

24a Maya Angelou

intelligent black women writers quiet for some years. But in the multicultural society in which we live, the contribution they are making to the broad literary tradition cannot go unnoticed. Several publishing companies have for some time encouraged black women to write.

America has had a longer history of racial struggle than Britain and has consequently a much more established literary tradition. Zora Neale Hurston, Alice Walker, Maya Angelou, Angela Davis, Toni Morrison and many other eminent black women writers speak out about experiences, attitudes and behaviours which contribute to nourish and keep black culture alive. Though it can be helpful to be interviewed and studied by the 'experts', there is nothing more useful than speaking for ourselves. These writers enable readers, both black and white, to learn about understanding others and encourage them to work towards a harmonious co-existence. They also provide for young black people an opportunity to develop a positive sense of their own cultural identity and enhance their perception of who they are. Beverley Bryan reminds us that:

> More and more Black women are able to sing, write and speak about the realities of being Black and female, rejecting the myths and stereotypes and reasserting those aspects of our lives which we have determined to be valid. (Beverley Bryan *et al*, *The Heart of the Race*, Virago, 1985)

25 Joan Riley

There are a number of black women in Britain who have contributed to this growing tradition: Grace Nichols, Joan Riley, Lauretta Ngcobo, Merle Collins, Jackie Kay, Janice Shinebourne, Marsha Prescod, Barbara Burford, Sandra Agard, Buchi Emecheta, Millie Murray, and many more published and unpublished black women writers, playwrights, biographers and poets. Their writings are based on personal experiences and historical themes with a particular emphasis on issues which bring a commonality and oneness to all black people, in communities, nationally and worldwide.

Only five years ago there was no Black Arts sector in Britain. One exists today, promoting all the different art forms from a black culture perspective. A Black Book Fair and Feminist Book Fair are held annually. A wide selection of black women's literature in the form of poetry, prose, journalism and plays is to be found alongside the other books by famous and new writers on the market. Afro-American books have been selling well on this side of the Atlantic, but black British-based women writers are often caught up in a web of having to produce material which conforms to a particular model before a publisher is found who will accept their books. Their writing about elements of their life which readers can relate to, like injustice, hope, humour, happiness, racism and pain, has sometimes to be forfeited in one way or another. When they are published, their books are often promoted in book shops and libraries on separate shelves for women, or Afro-Caribbean readers. This denies them the wide readership they might enjoy if they were simply promoted as good literature.

There are several feminist publishing houses who have provided a platform for black British-based writing to be published.

The setting up of a black women's press would be a liberating development for these women and would encourage more women to try and be published. They could finally have their feelings and thoughts published without the complications and restrictions which so often weigh them down. An attempt has been made by some black cooperatives and individuals to move in this direction but funding is required to make their efforts viable. What help relatives or friends can offer would only provide a temporary stop gap. It really needs big capital to ensure such a venture works. Something of this nature is very much needed.

Evidence

A What should be obvious to all those who are interested in Black cultural history is that Black women have always been involved in the creation and performance of our literature, especially oral literature. From time immemorial, we have been the undisputed practitioners of the art. Our involvement in this did not begin only when we changed to the scripted form of expression. We have been writing for a long time; it is now that these writings are beginning to come out into the open.
(Lauretta Ngcobo, *Let It Be Told*, Virago, 1988)

B Yuh hear 'bout?

Yuh hear bout di people dem arres
Fi bun dung di Asian people dem house?
Yuh hear bout di policeman dem lock up
Fi beat up di black bwoy widout a cause?
Yuh hear bout di MP dem sack because im refuse fi help
im coloured constituents in a dem fight 'gainst deportation?
Yuh no hear bout dem?
Me neida.

Did You Hear About?

Did you hear about the people they arrested
For burning down the Asian people's house?
Did you hear about the policeman they put in jail
For beating up the black boy without any cause?
Did you hear about the MP they sacked
because he refused to help
his black constituents in their fight
against deportation?
You didn't hear about them?
Me neither.
(Valerie Bloom, in *Let It Be Told*)

C Joan Riley, *The Unbelonging*, The Women's Press, 1985. A black novel describing the physical and mental traumas in the life of a black girl in England. Hyacinth, emigrating from Jamaica, suffers a loss of self-confidence because of her colour; in a society where 'whiteness' is the basis of acceptable beauty, she feels ugly and contemptuous of herself. 'Sometimes in her secret fantasies she would be swept off her feet by a rich, passionate stranger . . . . Always her hair would be blonde and flowing, her skin pale and white.'
(Reviewed in *A Reader's Guide to West Indian and Black British Literature*, Hansib Publishing and Rutherford Press, 1988)

D Before I could consider what I wanted to include in this piece, I first had to decide whether I wanted to write it. This is because, if I am honest, I have become quite cynical about Blackwomen producing a certain type of experiential writing that is too often marketed for a white target audience. Moreover, I had to come to terms with the problem that if the book was to be aimed at a wider audience that would include Black women, should I really write something that was negative, since so much of what Black women find available to read at the moment is of this kind. This is not to say that writings which concentrate on the negative aspects of our lives are invalid and should therefore be condemned; in fact I think such writings are very necessary as they illustrate to us just how resilient we are – such writings inspire us and give us strength. It is just that I feel that at times something positive has to be said also. This dilemma was resolved for me when I came to the conclusion that it is possible to turn negative experiences into positive strengths.

(Agnes Quashie, 'Coming of Age', in Joan Scanlon (ed.), *Surviving the Blues*, Virago, 1990)

Questions

1 What evidence is there in A and B of the oral origins of black women's writing? What value did this oral tradition have for future generations?

2 What does the reviewer of Joan Riley's *The Unbelonging* (C) pick out as an important theme in the book? Why do you think the author chose this theme?

3 Why do you think Agnes Quashie (D) was worried about the writings of black women in Britain? What do you think she means by 'it is possible to turn negative experiences into positive strengths'?

4 Why do you think more black British writers haven't become household names?

5 Visit your library and carry out a survey on the type of books which are read. Find out if your library keeps books written by black authors. If they do, try reading one of your choice.

CHAPTER 8

Black Women See New Horizons

Barbara Barlow (b. 14 December 1944)

Barbara Barlow is a Jamaican woman in her forties, who has lived in the North West of England for the past 23 years. She has three grown-up children and has worked for many years as a personal assistant secretary to a senior manager at a university. She was for many years a

mother and a housewife. If it was not for her mother paying her a visit from the Caribbean she would never have realized that she had the option to retrain in a new area, update her skills or even return to formal education. It took some time for Barbara to enroll on a Training Opportunities Scheme (TOPS) course for almost a year to improve her secretarial skills. Furthermore, she was also given a small allowance from the

26 Barbara Barlow in 1967

government to do this. Barbara recalls:

> I was amazed every time I got my Giro, someone was actually willing to pay me to do a course.

She derived a lot of joy from returning to college and, despite the fact that she was joining the last year of a two-year course, she managed exceptionally well and was pleasantly surprised at the progress she made. She applied for and got a job soon after leaving the course. It was not long before a job at the university came up. With some degree of reservation Barbara applied and was appointed.

Unfortunately, she never had the opportunity to update and receive training in appropriate areas. Her

27 Barbara Barlow in the Physics Department, Manchester University, 1989

work over the time increased both in terms of volume and the degree of responsibility she was given. This was not acknowledged for she found that, though she was left unsupervised to carry out the work, which she did to a high standard, the financial rewards have never matched the challenging workload. In 1990 she decided that she would resign and spend the next three years studying at the local polytechnic for a Bachelor of Arts Honours degree.

Barbara has decided to make an upward step to show to herself and her children that getting on is for the taking, providing the commitment is genuine. Her decision has given her the self-confidence to realize that, irrespective of her age, race, gender or social position, she has the ability to make her dream of some ten years become a reality.

Questions

1 Why do you think Barbara Barlow was unaware of the training possibilities open to her until her mother told her about them?

2 In what ways has Barbara Barlow taken her future into her own hands? Why is this still difficult for many black women to do?

We All Have a Dream

Black women of all ages and backgrounds have acquired a knowledge of what it takes to survive. In the early 1950s and 60s, when they had the courage to take the chance to leave their homelands and come to Britain, they encountered discrimination in its many forms as well as a different way of life. For some individuals it was all too much and the pressures they were confronted with eventually caused stress and serious illness. The majority, however, took control and endured the dominance of the host society.

Also, through the support, integrity, love and determination of their close relatives, friends and the wider community, they have developed the key to survival and living in Britain for over 30 years. Much of what has been written in this book has reflected on and drawn on examples from the lives of black women who became the first generation in Britain from the Commonwealth countries.

The close emotional bond between a mother and her children has been disrupted for many of these black women and their second generation offspring. Second generation children born in Britain often challenge the traditional beliefs of their parents. They find themselves torn between two different cultures, with different values, attitudes and customs. Eighty per cent of young black adults today between the ages of 16-24 were born in Britain to first generation families. The figures for those over 25 years is a mere three per cent. These young people are in the main black British citizens who have been brought up and educated in Britain and who know no other homeland. They are aware in general of the prejudice which affects key areas of their lives like employment, housing, and education.

In the main, black people are underrepresented in many professional sectors. We find it much harder to get jobs, and when we do have a job they are often below the level of our qualifications and experience. In the 1980s general job levels and incomes were still much higher in the white population than among black people. It is therefore not surprising that overall housing conditions for black people are lower than for whites. Such prejudice and conditions have had long-term effects on women's and children's physical and mental health, which they are having to get help for. The NHS and the welfare state are there to provide treatment and care for everyone. But inequalities exist in access to care and attention for black people there too. Many white people still believe that the black people in Britain are here to scrounge – to take advantage of the social security system and NHS. This book should have made it clear that nothing could be further from the truth.

Our experience of education in Britain differs from one socio-economic group to another. Black people have unfortunately not always benefited from the educational system. The 'white bias' that persists in education offers little opportunity to explore the positive contributions black people have made to society, literature and history, or for youngsters to explore together strategies for existing in a multiracial society.

The education I am receiving at school is not even slightly relevant to what I will have to encounter in the outside world. School is just a breeding ground for academics, and those who reject the system pay the price in low or no qualifications and a significant number of these pupils are black.
(Black British 15-year-old girl, 1990)

28 Valerie Amos, Chief Executive of the Equal Opportunities Commission

Education truly touches the lives and cultural values and attitudes of both young and old, black and white. We all need to realize and face the fact that racism in society's institutions still exists and that underlying racism needs to be exposed and tackled for what it signifies.

Needless to say, there is a glint of optimism about race relations in Britain for the future. There are many ambitious young and mature black women ready, willing and passionate about becoming their own success story. You only need to glance through some of the local and national ethnic newspapers to find examples of black women who have belied the persisting racist myth which suggests black people are unintelligent and lazy. It is no wonder that our black youth protests in rage about this image which they are daily fed. If we look for the good that is happening, it is there: examples of professional black women in the Stock Market, in the media, in politics, heading big organizations and institutions, running their own businesses – the list is endless. Black women in Britain are and can become the burning beacons of the future and still offer a quality contribution to the country they believe is home. Trying to keep determined women down only induces a stronger will to succeed.

So don't ask me where I've come from, ask me where I am going.
(West Indian proverb)

Evidence

A When my daughter was leaving school in the late sixties she felt that black women only got jobs as cleaners . . .
(Doris Braithwaite, Birmingham)

B Mity Ampona is Surrey University's media and communications officer. She says she's typical of her friends and many other women she meets in resenting the way that the growing numbers of British-bred ABC1 black women are resolutely ignored by the media. 'There's a whole class of black women – outnumbering black men – who hold down good jobs right across the strata of professions. They're very strong, they're intelligent, they own their own homes, control their own economic situation, have good friends . . . I see reflections of myself in the streets all the time.'

But although Ampona does not want to lose her working class roots, she is unhappy that she doesn't see herself or her friends reflected in the magazines she reads or in the advertisements she watches.

29 Black women have often been in the forefront of community action

(Stella Orakwue, 'High income low profile', *The Guardian*, 7 November 1990)

C Black parents occupy nursery school
by Shekhar Bhatia

Angry black parents were occupying a London nursery school today after ordering the white matron to leave. The takeover of the Clapton Park Nursery Day School, in Hackney, followed a dispute involving the matron, a black nursery assistant and Hackney Council's social services. The nursery – which is attended by 33 black children and two white children – has been boycotted by white members of the kitchen and teaching staff in support of the matron. The protesters say that they have taken over the nursery to try to persuade the council to employ black staff in management positions. A spokeswoman for the protesters said that the three senior management positions of matron, deputy matron and third in charge are all filled by white people. 'We do not feel this is appropriate and good for the majority of the children,' she said. 'We want the black children at the nursery to grow up believing that black people

can hold positions of responsibility.'
(*Evening Standard*, 27 September 1985)

D One important thing is the campaigns. Wherever there is an Asian community you will find people are campaigning over the injustice and racism which is destroying someone's life – over deportation or someone being arrested for defending their family or community from racial attack. (Because as you know racists are never, ever arrested . . .) Anwar Ditta won her right to bring her children into this country after five years of struggle and there are others who campaigned and won . . . and a lot of Asian girls were involved. As you said, the stereotype of youth is male but the thing is it is much harder for girls to be politically involved. It's not just because of our families but also the really macho atmosphere around everything political. In some campaigns that has started to change a bit. When the whole community is involved it also brings the parents and young people closer together . . . . Also, if you were writing now I think you would have mentioned the black women's groups. They organise campaigns and also provide a lot of support to women in the community. It is hard to imagine what it must have been like before they existed.
(Ayesha, interviewed in Amrit Wilson, *Finding a Voice: Asian Women in Britain*, Virago, 1984)

Questions

1 How have black women's expectations for their futures changed since the 1960s?

2 Why is Mity Ampona unhappy with the media in Britain? Why do you think we see so few professional black women in the media?

3 Why were the parents in C occuping the nursery? Why is it important for children to see black adults in professional jobs?

4 Changes for the better in black women's lives in Britain have not just happened on their own – they are the result of the struggles and campaigns of individuals and women's groups. What do you think black women still have to fight for?

Timeline

3rd century AD	African soldiers among Roman troops occupying Britain.
15th-18th centuries	Black people lived as slaves and servants in Britain.
1775-83	Black slaves recruited into British army and navy during American War of Independence.
1833	Abolition of slavery in Britain.
1853-56	Mary Seacole nursed wounded soldiers during Crimean War.
1905	Aliens Act passed by British government to control immigration.
1914-18	Eight divisions of the British West Indian Regiment served in the First World War.
1919	Race riots over employment of black people.
1939-45	100,000 black personnel served in the Second World War.
1948	Creation of National Health Service.
1950s	Large influx of black immigrants to Britain.
1950-54	McCarthy Era in the USA.
1952	McCarren Walter Act restricted immigration of British West Indians to the USA.
1958	First Notting Hill Carnival organized. *West Indian Gazette* founded.
1960	ANC and Pan African Congress outlawed in South Africa.
1962	Commonwealth Immigrants Act.
1968	Enoch Powell made 'rivers of blood' speech against black immigration.
1970s	Development of Black Power movement.
1976	Race Relations Act.
1976-78	Grunwick strike.
1977	Commission for Racial Equality established.
1987	Diane Abbott elected first black woman MP.

Books for further reading

Beverley Bryan *et al, The Heart of the Race: Black Women's Lives in Britain*, Virago, 1985

Angela Davis, *Women, Race and Class*, The Women's Press, 1982

Elyse Dodgson, *Motherland: West Indian Women to Britain in the 1950s*, Heinemann Educational, 1984

Peter Fryer, *Staying Power: The History of Black People in Britain*, Pluto Press, 1984

M. Mac An Ghaill, *Young, Gifted and Black*, Open University Press, 1988

Lauretta Ngcobo, *Let It Be Told: Black Women Writers in Britain*, Virago, 1987

A. Osler, *Speaking Out: Black Girls in Britain*, Virago, 1987

Amrit Wilson, *Finding a Voice: Asian Women in Britain*, Virago, 1984

Index